The Joy of Being a Woman
. . . And What a Man Can Do

HARPER JUBILEE BOOKS

The Joy of Being a Woman
...And What a Man Can Do

INGRID TROBISCH

HARPER & ROW, PUBLISHERS
New York, Hagerstown, San Francisco, London

THE JOY OF BEING A WOMAN. Copyright © 1975 by Ingrid Trobisch. All rights reserved. Printed in the United States of America. No part of this book may be used or reproduced in any manner whatsoever without written permission except in the case of brief quotations embodied in critical articles and reviews. For information address Harper & Row, Publishers, Inc., 10 East 53rd Street, New York, N.Y. 10022. Published simultaneously in Canada by Fitzhenry & Whiteside Limited, Toronto.

A HARPER JUBILEE BOOK

Library of Congress Cataloging in Publication Data

Trobisch, Ingrid Hult.
    The joy of being a woman . . . and what a man can do.
    (Harper jubilee books; HJ 13)
    Bibliography: p.
    1. Marriage. 2. Sex in marriage. 3. Femininity (Psychology) 4. Women—Health and hygiene. I. Title.
HQ734.T846   261.8′34′27   75-9324
ISBN 0-06-068448-8 pbk.

---

79 10 9 8 7

To my "doula"
who taught me
that in order to love
you must first let yourself be loved

Contents

Foreword

". . . and what a man can do"

One of these things, and certainly a pleasant one for me, is to write a short preface to my wife's book. It is my genuine wish that many husbands will consider making an investment of time and effort to read this book as their contribution toward enriching their marriages and also as a visible sign that they love their wives and thus themselves. The Apostle Paul says: "He who loves his wife loves himself" (Eph. 5:28).

Actually what Ingrid presents in her book is a synopsis of the main realms of experience in the life of a married woman: sexual fulfillment, fertility, pregnancy, childbirth, nursing, and finally menopause and maturity.

It is the tendency of our time that these realms are treated separately by individual specialists, and thus are often torn apart.

My wife seeks to bring together here that which belongs together. She shows that these realms of experience affect each other and are interrelated just like the cog wheels of a delicate instrument.

One cannot divide them up just as one cannot divide up the person experiencing them. The human being is essentially indivisible—an "individual." Therefore, in order to help the person to become and remain human, it is absolutely essential to view these realms altogether.

Much of what my wife writes here she has learned from world experts—each chapter has been inspired by a different authority. But she has also learned from her own experience as the wife of a difficult husband and as a mother of five children, as well as from personal, confidential talks with numerous people from different cultures and continents.

Many of these talks we experienced together, counseling as a couple with another couple, for we believe that this is the most effective and promising method of marriage counseling. While I have presented, from a husband's point of view, what we learned from these talks in my books, expecially in *I Married You* (Harper & Row), I am so glad that Ingrid now presents what she has learned from a wife's point of view.

Most best-selling sex manuals of our time are written by and for men, within the narrow horizon of a man's perspective. But, as Lillian Roxon has put it, "The warm and loving book by the warm and loving woman has yet to be written."

I believe it can be truly stated that the message my wife proclaims in this book has never been said before, at least not in this way and in this form.

Walter Trobisch

A Personal Note to the Reader

I enjoy being a woman. Not that it has always been easy. In every period of my life, I have had to learn it anew—first as a single and professional woman until I was 27, then as a wife, childless for the first three years of our marriage, and finally as the mother of our two daughters and three sons.

My experiences come out of different cultures. I grew up and was educated in the United States. I then lived and worked for twelve years in Africa. For more than a decade I have made my home in Europe. In each continent and situation the joy of being a woman has meant something different for me.

There are two kinds of women's movements today: those which try to eradicate the differences between the sexes and urge women to be like men, and those which fully appreciate the uniqueness of womanhood. I want to dedicate this book to the latter group. I want to help the liberated woman to retain her femininity. "Aimer être femme!" "To love being a woman!" That's our first and uncontestable allegiance," says Marie Défossez in her book, *Vivre au féminin*. It is just as important that the man can say with his whole heart, "I enjoy being a man." For without emancipated man, there will never be emancipated woman.

That is why I have written this book just as much for men as for women. It is my hope that there will be courageous couples who will read and discuss it together and thus find a new basis for dialogue, that of "bibliotherapy."

What about the single reader? I feel that all I have said about self-acceptance applies to each one of us, whether married, not yet married, or single. As my brother wrote after reading the manuscript, "Your statement, 'If I do not live in peace with my body, I do not live in peace with my Creator' has such a profound meaning. If both women and men could really make this statement in the affirmative, *at least* 50% of all physician visits would be cancelled."

His comment after reading the second chapter was, "Something needs to be said to all the wonderful people in the world who never experience the joy of heterosexual love . . ." I would like to pay them a tribute here, just as I would those many husbands and wives who because of illness or other circumstances live in an unfulfilled marriage—at least as far as their sexual lives are concerned.

There is something sparkling and radiant about a woman or a man who does not deny their sexuality, but who pours it out in love to others. I see in them the picture of Mary of Bethany who poured her bottle of costly perfume on Jesus' feet and then wiped them with her hair. (In African cultures, a girl about to be married gives her fiancé a decorated gourd in the shape of a vase or a bottle as a symbol of her feminine sexuality.) Mary's action in pouring out the bottle of costly perfume could symbolize this precious gift. That she used her long hair, a sexual symbol in Jewish culture, to wipe

Jesus' feet, shows that she was not afraid of her womanhood.

No man will ever be able to satisfy completely the innermost desires of a woman's heart for love, beauty and shelteredness. I believe it is possible to live a full life, whether single or married, in spite of unfulfilled desires. We can only look to the One who says: "My purpose is to give life in all its fulness" (John 10:10).

Acknowledgments

This book would never have been written if a single woman had not challenged me to discover the joys of being a woman and if she had not accompanied me emotionally during my first and each succeeding pregnancy, rejoicing in the birth of our children as if they had been her own. She was my "doula", the one who "mothers the mother." When I asked her at a later date, "How do you learn how to love?" her answer without hesitation was, "By letting yourself be loved." Because she has shown me so specifically God's love, I can believe that He loves and accepts me too.

I am grateful to each one of the authors listed in the bibliography. Often in my reading, I found myself conversing with them about each new discovery I made. "That makes sense!" I said. It was the joy of learning by insight.

I want to thank the couples who have allowed me to use quotations from their personal letters. Also thanks to Dorothea Vosgerau with whom I spent precious hours discussing the contents of each chapter. She has the qualities of a super-executive and yet knows how to mother without smothering.

Special thanks go to the medical doctors who have read the manuscript and given their helpful criticism and corrections: my brother John Hult, Marsh Matthews, Josef Roetzer and Rudolf Vollman.

Much of the information in chapter two I have learned from the newsletters and personal contacts with the Couple to Couple movements in France, U.S.A., and Canada. For permission to use the illustrations from *Love and Life* on pages 35, 40, 66, my thanks to Serena, Inc., Ottawa, Canada and especially Arthur and Connie Johnson. Also thanks to Dr. Robert Bradley for permission to use the illustration on page 89 adapted from his book, *Husband-Coached Childbirth.*

To the wonderful girls who lived with our family during this year and who helped complete and type the manuscript, Elizabeth Goldhor and Marie de Putron, I want to express my deep thanks.

And finally, I want to thank our children. They have encouraged me and made my life rich and full, each one in his or her own individual way. To their father, who also fathered this book, I give my heartfelt thanks—not only for his patience and help in this project—but for accepting me without condition throughout the years of our marriage and for giving me the freedom to be me.

Ingrid Trobisch
A-4880 St. Georgen,
Austria

The Joy of Being a Woman
... And What a Man Can Do

I

Self-acceptance—The Key

Women will not be freed by trying to be like men. The challenge of liberation is more difficult. It is also more precious and rewarding. The key is that women accept themselves in their uniqueness as women.

In his essay, "The Acceptance of Oneself," Romano Guardini writes the following:

"At the root of all things lies the act of accepting myself. I must agree to be who I am. I must accept the qualifications which I have. I must accept the limitations set for me. . . . The clarity and courageousness of this acceptance provides the basis of all life."[1]

This means that the task of self-acceptance applies to men as well as women. It is hard work because it is not something with which we are born. We have to learn it during the course of life and the learning process is not easy. Just how difficult it is becomes clear when we ask ourselves the following questions: have I accepted myself with my gifts? With my limitations? With my dangers? Have I accepted my age, my state of health, my economic situation? Have I accepted the way I look?

Do I say "Yes" to my marriage or to my being single? Above all, have I accepted my sexuality, my gender? Have I accepted my femininity or masculinity?

A professional man in his best years was asked: "What is your secret? How do you live in such peace with yourself?" He answered without hesitation: "It is because my wife lives in harmony with herself." A husband can accept his masculinity only if his wife accepts her femininity. Living and accepting one's own gender is the greatest help which the sexes can give to each other. I cannot accept my partner unless I accept myself. I cannot love my partner unless I love myself.

Jesus points to this secret when He commands us to love our neighbor not *instead* of ourselves, but *as* ourselves. In this way He makes self-love in the sense of self-acceptance the yardstick for our attitude toward our neighbor.

On the other hand we can learn to accept ourselves only when we are accepted by others. We can acquire the ability to love ourselves only if we allow ourselves to be loved by others.

What if this does not happen? Do we remain hopelessly alone if such love is withheld?

At this point it becomes clear that the question of self-acceptance is basically a question of faith.

In his Epistle to the Romans, the apostle Paul wrote: "Accept one another, as Christ has accepted you for the glory of God" (Romans 15:7).

In Jesus Christ we are unconditionally accepted. In Jesus Christ we are unconditionally loved. In Him is the source from which any deficit of love in our lives can be filled. In Him is the source of power which can enable us to love and accept ourselves—and thus our neighbor.

I write this book as a personal testimony of my own acceptance by Jesus Christ. It is my hope that this will be conveyed through each page of the book. Only because I know myself accepted and loved by Christ, am I able to accept myself fully and to say with my whole heart, "I enjoy being a woman."

Self-acceptance of the Body

Both men and women have to work on self-acceptance. It seems to me, though, that it is harder for a woman to accept herself than it is for a man.

One reason is evident in the conscious or unconscious discrimination against women in our society. The other reason may be that in her life as a person, the woman is more related to her body than the man.

Her physical being is more complicated than that of a man. For him the sexual experience is simpler and more straightforward. His function in procreation is certainly less complicated than the event of conception for her. The experience of a menstrual cycle, of pregnancy, birth, and breastfeeding remain foreign to a man, who in the words of the German poet Rainer Maria Rilke, "is not pulled underneath the surface of life by the heaviness of bodily fruit."

Therefore self-acceptance for a woman is to a greater degree physical self-acceptance. What she has to accept weighs heavier. Women who know themselves to be accepted by Christ are no exception in this struggle.

One reason why Christian women especially have such a hard time accepting themselves, including their bodies, is because the idea still prevails that the spiritual and mental areas of our lives are somehow closer to God, more pleasing to him and more "Christian" than the physical realm. The Bible, which calls the body the "temple of the Holy Spirit" (I Corinthians 6:19), says the contrary: the more authentic our faith is, the more we are able to live in peace with our bodies. The more I succeed in accepting myself as a physical creature, the more I am able to live in harmony and peace with myself.

This is true also for my peace with God. I believe that the relationship I have to my body is reflected in my relationship to God. If I do not live in peace with my body, I do not live in peace with my Creator.

Consequently, the physical experiences of the woman will be very much in the foreground in this book. I know from many conversations with women from all over the world that it is just their bodies which often make it difficult for them to accept themselves and to love themselves as women.

This is true not only for the married woman in the full flower of her years, but also for the woman during and after menopause. It is just as true for the single woman and for the adolescent girl. Every woman has to learn anew in every phase of her life to understand what happens in her body biologically and to live in harmony with herself.

Dr. Paul Tournier from Switzerland tells in his book *A Place for You* about one of his patients who, when she entered a hotel room, either covered up all the mirrors in her room or turned them around. She couldn't stand to see herself—especially when she was naked. She had not accepted her body, had not yet learned to be thankful for it. She had not yet learned "to put her arms around herself."

In contrast I think of the poster depicting a little naked girl stretching out her arms, as if to embrace not only herself but the world. She is standing on the shore of a vast ocean. The caption underneath says: "To be nobody else!"

It is a well-known fact today that spiritual conflicts can affect a person physically. But we have not yet drawn the opposite conclusion, namely, that physical conflicts can hinder and disturb our spiritual life.

Therefore, once more: for this *spiritual* reason, I want to talk in this book predominantly about the *physical* experiences of being a woman. I agree with those women of today who underline the fact that "body education is core education. Our bodies are the physical bases from which we move out into the world; ignorance, uncertainty—even, at worst, shame—about our physical selves create in us an alienation from ourselves that keeps us from being the whole people that we could be."[2]

The physical experiences of being a woman are many layered, especially when we think of all that happens to her in reproduction. In comparison with a man, who knows only one experience—the experience of the physical union—the woman has several, all of which are related to each other and intertwined like the petals in a rose. These interrelated experiences will be discussed in the following pages: (1) the wife's joy in sexual response; (2) living in harmony with the cycle of fertility; (3) the wonderful time of expecting; (4) childbirth—a marital experience; (5) the motherly art of breastfeeding; (6) menopause—a chance for a new beginning.

II
The Wife's Joy in Sexual Response

Joy—Only for the Husband?

... this body ... tormented.

In the burning coals of our union, it is so seldom that it reaches the goal—that it begins to vibrate!

Even though I desire it with all my heart, and want it with all my will, nothing happens.

It is like a motor which refuses to start—or it starts, and then turns over for a long time, but without getting any place.

I hate myself. I'm beginning to fear these nights which do not really help us to find each other!

John seems to be satisfied. Is he really?

I hide from him the dissatisfaction which he does not know how to satisfy.

Joy—is it something meant only for the husband?

But of what use is joy that is not shared? Tension mounts within me. Toward what end? I don't know.[1]

Many women all over the world will echo in their hearts the feelings which Ancelle, a French author, expresses in this poem. She tries to put into words the suffering and fine torture of a wife who does not reach sexual fulfillment in her marriage. There are many examples in literature all over the world which even give the impression that this is the case for the majority of women. I know that often in Africa, as well as in other cultures, the idea is foreign that a wife can find joy and fulfillment in sexual relations with her husband. Very often sexual pleasure is thought of as something which is reserved for the man. In spite of all the literature to the contrary in our culture, I often wonder if this still unconsciously does not play a part in the thinking of many.

The Bible does not agree with this idea. Sexual joy *is* a gift of God to both husband and wife. I would like to encourage those wives who may feel like Ancelle to have hope. Don't we have a God "who is able to give us richly all things to enjoy" (I Timothy 6:17)? May I share some practical suggestions which have been helpful to many?

Again the secret lies in the self-acceptance of the woman as a woman and especially in saying Yes to her body with its special ways of experiencing life. I must draw attention briefly to some of the differences between man and woman, for it is just in these differences that the richness of creation is expressed. The task we face is to say Yes without reserve to being different, for only then can we complete each other, give to each other, and become truly one with each other.

Arrow and Mirror

Words and pictures can only touch upon the secret of becoming one while yet remaining two individuals. No words can grasp the secret completely; no illustration can describe it adequately.

My husband once gave a lecture in Africa about marriage and what it means for a husband and wife, who are different in their natures, to become one person. I recall an elderly African pastor who stood up in the crowded hall and in a solemn voice, trembling with emotion, asked: "How is this possible? How can two become one?" The answer is not simple. Probably it cannot be explained—only experienced in awe and amazement.

In order to give a hint at what this oneness while yet remaining two individuals means, Dr. Bovet of Switzerland has suggested that the husband be likened to the *head* of the marriage person, while the wife be likened to the *heart*. This is certainly not an evaluation in a patriarchal sense, but it points to the service which both partners render to each other in their marriage, each one with specific gifts. The husband's gift often tends more to thinking than to feeling. When a decision must be made, he thinks it over carefully and reasons it out. Then he will say, "This is what I am convinced of. . . . This is what I think." The wife, on the other hand, because of her greater gift of intuition, is apt to say, "This is what I sense is right. . . . This is what I feel."

Of course, these illustrations do not put forth an absolute truth; rather, they hint at something relative. A man certainly can also "feel" just as a woman can also "think." The same is true of the other comparisons which Dr. Bovet uses to describe the differences in the function of man and wife. He likens the husband to the captain of a boat, while the wife is the one who takes care of the passengers in the boat. The husband is the architect and builder of the house, while it is the wife who is the interior decorator, who lightens it up with her presence, changes the bare walls into a cozy home, and thus fulfills one of her special gifts—that of creating an atmosphere.

The male medical symbol is a circle with an arrow, used in ancient times as the sign of the planet Mars. A man is like an arrow with his interest pointing outward toward the world. The medical symbol for the female is that of a mirror, taken from the sign of the planet Venus. I like to think of the wife reflecting back and responding to the love which she receives from her husband.

Grassfire and Charcoal Embers

These differences between men and women are also reflected in the difference in their sexual experience. The Bible uses here the verb "to know," indicating that it is more than something physical. It is an event which involves mind and spirit as well. But precisely because of this, it is indispensable that the physical process be understood in its whole depth and meaning. Otherwise it is impossible "to know" each other in the full sense of this biblical term.

For the man the sexual act is something which happens within a limited time. His physical desire is quickly aroused and just as quickly satisfied. He does not need a long preparation. In a relatively short time he reaches the climax and after that he can turn immediately to other things and interests. Like an arrow he heads straight for his goal. His curve of pleasure goes up steeply and when the climax is reached returns almost instantly to zero.

For the woman, this is quite different. She needs

much more time. Her curve of pleasure rises gently and gradually. She experiences the climax not as one point, but more like a plateau. From this plateau she descends slowly and reluctantly.

One of my African sisters, Madame Ernestine Banyolak, found the following comparison to illustrate the different time element of man and woman: a man's experience is like a fire of dry leaves, easily kindled, flaring up suddenly and dying down just as quickly. The experience of the woman is, on the other hand, like a fire of glowing charcoal. Her husband has to blow on the coals with loving patience. Once the blaze is burning brightly, it will keep on glowing and radiating warmth for a long time.

That is why it is so hard for a woman to understand that the man's experience has a definite beginning and an end. For her the sexual act is, strictly speaking, not an action with a definite beginning and ending. For her this atmosphere of love is always there to a certain degree. Her thinking and feeling are related to her husband even if she is working, preparing a meal, cleaning the house, doing the laundry, or shopping. She cannot separate her body from her soul. That which she feels inside is the same which she expresses outwardly.

Longing for love and sexual desire are a unity for her and penetrate her whole being. That is why, when her sexual desire is fulfilled, she has almost supernatural strength. She can easily master the small problems of her daily life. Peace and fulfillment give her a contagious and radiant joy of life.

It is for the sake of this joy of life that I want to talk very frankly and concretely about the experience of orgasm. I certainly do not maintain that the happiness of marriage depends upon this experience alone, as is often claimed in popular and cheap literature. I know too that different women have different levels of feeling.

There are women who have never experienced what I am now going to describe—or at least have not experienced it in the same way and who, in spite of this, live in harmony with themselves. If so, they should not think of themselves as sexual cripples. Neither should they reproach their husbands or develop guilt feelings. I do not want to take their peace away from them. But perhaps I can open up to some couples a new dimension of mutual knowledge and oneness.

Orgasm is not the condition of a good marriage. But it can and may be the fruit of a good marriage. And it is certainly a fruit worth aspiring for! God wants to give this fruit to all couples, and those who miss it because they are literally too lazy to work at their marriages or to inform themselves about the way they are created are guilty. I cannot say this loudly and clearly enough, especially to those Christians who believe themselves too "devout" to study such a "worldly" matter. They do not take the words seriously which they confess every Sunday in the creed: "I believe in God, the Creator," who has created them as they are.

Wading Pool and Mountain Lake

For me there is no doubt that a woman has two different ways of experiencing sexual pleasure. The one experience I would like to compare with that of a child splashing around in a wading pool, where it finds a certain satisfaction even though it cannot yet swim. The other experience is like diving and swimming in the deep and clear waters of a mountain lake.

The more superficial way consists of the manipulation of the clitoris. The clitoris is located at the upper end of the vulva, above the female urinary opening, where the folds of skin called labia minora, or minor lips, meet. The clitoris is shaped like the penis, but is much smaller. It is usually ¾ to 1½ inches long and is very sensitive to the touch because it has many nerve endings. The meaning of the Latin word *clitoris* is "little key." It provides pleasure during foreplay. However, orgasm can be induced by the stimulation of the clitoris. It is described by women as superficial, a nervous contraction resulting in a sharp climax, but which is not fully satisfying. It is felt along the surface of the body, as something outside, but not deep within the body. It can be stimulated either by oneself (masturbation) or by one's partner, which is called deep petting.

If by either of these ways a girl gets used to release by clitoral orgasm, her sexuality may become fixated to this form of sexual pleasure and she may find it much more difficult later on to mature to the vaginal experience. She is likely to remain at an auto-erotical phase—deep petting is actually only a mutual form of masturbation. In not learning the use of sexuality for the purpose of communication, she gets used to transferring tension immediately into pleasure and she loses an energy which she needs in order to find her true identity as a woman. Therefore the ability of self-acceptance is endangered through the superficial clitoral experience. The swimming in the deep mountain lake, however, is not possible without self-acceptance.

The maturing process of female sexuality consists in the transfer of the sexual feeling from the clitoral area to the vaginal area. Women who progress from one experience to the other judge the first one as childish and immature. "For the first time I feel like a woman" they say, after the fulfilling experience of a vaginal orgasm. It is described by women as being profound, something deeper which involves the entire body and provides for the wife a rich and deep release and satisfaction.

Masters and Johnson have tried to prove with scientific methods that there is no difference between clitoral and vaginal orgasm as far as the purely physiological symptoms are concerned. What could not be measured by their methods, however, was the beauty and the mystery of the emotional experience.

Just as one cannot record the beauty of a symphony by recording sound waves or measure the beauty of a sunrise as seen from a mountaintop by scientific methods, so it is impossible to measure the depth of joy, closeness, security, and oneness which a wife experiences in total union—body, mind, and spirit—with her husband.

In a very interesting study reported in *Modern Woman*, Dr. Leah Schaefer comes to the same conclusion. She states that the physiological experience of orgasm was identical regardless of the source of stimulation in the woman she interviewed, but emotionally their feeling of satisfaction or dissatisfaction was very different. One woman said to her: "To me an orgasm which is involved with vaginal penetration is by far the most satisfying . . . it feels much more fulfilling and complete. . . . I'm very conscious of the spasm part of the orgasm—of the feeling that once it starts there is no way to stop it, but to localize where the feeling seems to take place is kind of difficult since it seems to reverberate over my entire body."[2]

Basically the clitoral experience is by nature a masculine experience because the clitoris would have developed into the penis if the baby girl had been a boy. Some leaders of the women's movement deny the vaginal experience in accordance with their denial of women's femininity. It is therefore only logical that they deny everything which a woman has in her own right and consequently invite women to masturbate when they want to experience sexual pleasure in order to become independent from men and at the same time "emancipate" themselves to a masculine experience. If they only knew the deeper sexual pleasure they could experience by learning to accept and love themselves as women.

I have found very helpful that which Dr. and Mrs. Joseph Bird write in their book *The Freedom of Sexual Love*. They use the word "total" in order to describe the mature female orgasm. Here is their description:

> . . . perhaps the word *total* would be more descriptive of the mature female orgasm. It is an orgasm which starts deep within her body—subjectively, at least, in the vagina—and extends, as it increases in intensity, to every part of her body, seemingly to the tips of her fingernails. At its peak, her whole being seems to dissolve and she experiences an indescribable feeling of fulfillment and transcendence. She feels a loss of her ego boundaries as her entire being flows into him. It is an experience of such profoundness and meaning that no analogy is adequate to describe it, an experience which pervades and affects every aspect of her relationship with her husband, and one which makes the male orgasm seem almost rudimentary by comparison.[3]

The Kegel Muscle

When I was looking for a way to help those women who suffered because they had never had such an experience, I met Dr. Arnold Kegel in Los Angeles, at that time clinical professor of gynecology at the University of Southern California School of Medicine. Shortly before his death he asked my husband and myself personally to pass on in our Family Life Seminars that which he had discovered to be of help to so many.

He made this discovery in a strange way. As a surgeon he very often had to treat women who suffered from urinary incontinence because of a weak muscle condition. He developed an exercise for his patients in order to relieve this condition. It happened time and again that patients who returned for a check-up after their treatment reported to him an unexpected side-effect of his therapy: for the first time they had experienced a total orgasm.

This discovery motivated Dr. Kegel to dedicate the rest of his life to the study of the pubococcygeus muscle, which in medical literature is often called the Kegel muscle.

There are many women who have a good marriage who have said Yes to their femininity, who know the secret of self-acceptance, who are also deeply loved by their husbands, yet who have experienced very little of what Joseph and Lois Bird have described as total orgasm.

If such women would have a medical check-up, their doctors might tell them that the band of muscles which controls the opening of the bladder, the vagina, and the rectum is too weak and too slack. Dr. Kegel discovered the greatest source of sexual sensation to be just beyond the upper edge of this muscle inside the vagina. Many women lack full sexual response because this upper portion of the muscle is not well-developed. Here are the nerve endings which cause the band of muscle to contract during orgasm.

Imagine the cross-section of the vagina like the face of a clock, with the numeral 12 pointing to the pubic bone and the numeral 6 to the coccyx, or tail bone. The place of the strongest sexual sensation is on the right side and the left side, a little below the center, where the 4 and the 8 of the clock's face would be.

It is a fact that many women—Dr. Kegel estimates them to be as many as two-thirds—have very little va-

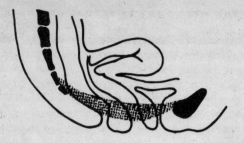

Fig. 1 The pubococcygeus muscle with good tone and proper position.

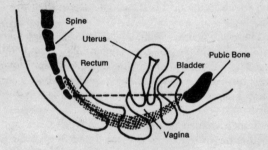

Fig. 2 The pubococcygeus (Kegel) muscle with poor tone and position. Note the sinking of the uterus and widening vagina due to weak support.

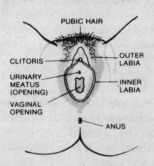

Fig. 3 External female sex organs (Vulva).

ginal sensation in sexual intercourse because the pubococcygeus muscle is not fully developed.

A Very Simple Exercise

Dr. Paul Popenoe, founder of the American Institute of Family Relations in Los Angeles, who worked closely with Dr. Kegel, has proposed a very simple exercise to strengthen this important muscle. He reports that in a series of over a thousand cases of sexually unsatisfied women who asked for help, 65 percent gained relief simply by practicing this exercise. (Among the other 35 percent were those who had deep-rooted emotional problems as well as some cases of serious physical disease.)[4]

Dr. Popenoe gives the following suggestions for training this muscle:

The Kegel muscle can be strengthened by "pulling up" on it as if making a strong effort to shut off or hold back the flow of urine. A wife who lacks satisfactory sensation in the vagina or who is unable to have orgasm, should practice this regularly, keeping her feet spread a little apart. She may do so for a few minutes at a time, half a dozen times a day, even when she is engaged in some of her housework. Or she may count the contractions and plan on, say 300 a day, divided into groups of 50 each. Strengthening the muscles in this way usually narrows and lengthens the vagina and pulls the organs of the pelvis up into their proper position. If the wife suffers from low backache, which is relieved when she is lying down, or if she has a tendency to lose a little urine when she strains, sneezes, or even laughs, there is a strong suggestion that the Kegel muscle is weak and the exercise just mentioned often gives relief.[5]

Dr. Kegel suggests that each voiding of urine be an opportunity for exercise. When passing urine a woman should try to stop and restart: on-off, on-off.

In order not to forget this exercise, one woman wrote little notes to herself as a reminder and put them in different places in her apartment—in the bedroom, bathroom, even in the living room and above the kitchen sink. Just the one word, "Remember!" When her neighbor who was in the process of getting a divorce came over to visit her, she wanted to know the reason for all those notes. After she had received the information, she, too, started to exercise. The divorce never took place.

"It is a rare woman," says Dr. Popenoe, "who cannot heighten her sexual adequacy through this understanding and technique, usually to a considerable extent. We now try to give this information to every woman we see professionally. We believe that this is a key to good adjustment."[6]

My husband and I have counseled with many women in Africa who were clitoridectomized either as babies or at the age of puberty as a part of their initiation rites. This is called female circumcision and the clitoris is removed either in whole or in part by a primitive operation done under unsanitary conditions. Of course the operation can be disastrous, resulting in excessive bleeding as well as scarred tissue which may cause complications in childbirth later. It is also absolutely unnecessary for hygienic reasons. Yet it was our experience that these women who had undergone this cruel operation could be helped in arriving at a vaginal orgasm through exercising their Kegel muscle, thus learning an awareness of function. If such women can be helped, is there not hope for every healthy woman regardless of her age?

A woman of sixty, herself a marriage counselor, learned how to do the exercises. A month later, she reported exuberantly, for the first time in forty years of marriage she had experienced a total orgasm.

From this example we can also learn that there is no reason to believe that the ability to experience sexual pleasure ceases with menopause. There are many couples sixty and more years of age who experience joy and fulfillment in their sexual relations.

By the way, many symptoms point out that there is a relationship between the condition of the Kegel muscle and the physical and emotional well-being of any woman. It has been reported that in England a prolapsed uterus is found frequently among women suffering from depression. The condition of the Kegel muscle and the pelvic floor can reflect the way these women feel about life—sometimes the bottom actually is falling out. (Sometimes this muscle has been so badly damaged by a "tearing" traumatic delivery that the bottom literally has "fallen out." The exercise certainly couldn't hurt such a woman, but a good gynecological surgeon might be able to repair the muscle even years later.)

Dr. J. P. Greenhill, professor of gynecology at Chicago's Cook County School of Medicine, and editor of the *Yearbook of Obstetrics and Gynecology*, says: "In all the reports on the use of the Kegel technique there has never been any question of its safety for any woman. And for surprising numbers of women, its benefits, both sexually and medically, are likely to be great indeed."[7]

Peace in Deep Union

Now I must add a word for the husband; otherwise one might get the impression that the woman alone is responsible for a successful sexual union. That would be just as wrong as to claim that it is up to the man alone to carry the responsibility for satisfying his wife sexually and that unless he succeeds in doing it, he isn't really a man.

Of course, the cooperation of both is necessary. Both carry equal responsibility for what is experienced in the act of love. If her experience is like the glowing embers of charcoal and his like a quick-burning fire of dry leaves, then the husband's contribution should be to prolong the act as long as possible. One survey in the United States has shown that the average woman reaches orgasm after five minutes of intercourse, with some 12 percent needing at least ten minutes. On the other hand, the average man reaches orgasm in less than two minutes, with a large number of men completing the act in less than a minute. This again sheds a light on the words by Ancelle which I quoted at the beginning of this chapter. Is there a way for the husband better to control the timing of his orgasm? Knowing this would relieve him from tension and fearfulness.

First of all I would give the husband the same advice as the wife. He too should practice the same muscle exercise. It hurts no one. (Pediatricians, by the way, advise it for children who suffer from bed-wetting. The earlier they start, the better it is.) A mature man with a trained muscle will be able to tense it in the decisive moment and thus delay ejaculation. Premature ejaculation is one of the greatest hindrances to the sexual fulfillment of a wife.

Another help for the man is that he remain motionless after penetration, until the first wave of excitement dies down. Resting in deep union with his wife means peace for the husband. He should really enjoy this moment, and a loving wife will gladly give him this peace.

The movements will then start slowly and gently and the wife should be active as well. With a trained muscle, she can embrace her husband's penis with her vagina as if she wanted to hug him. It is important to know that it is not the back and forth movements which help the wife the most, but the gentle pressure sideways towards the walls of the vagina where the 4 and the 8 of the face of the clock come, as described earlier.

Again Ronald Deutsch says: "Many couples think vigorous thrusting is the expected technique in intercourse, perhaps because this becomes the instinct as orgasm nears. But friction, while masking sensation for the woman, overstimulates the man."[8]

Restfulness and gentleness provide help for both partners. In this way not only the wife is helped to find a deeper fulfillment. A new realm of experience opens up for the husband also. With every moment with which he is able to prolong the sexual union, his self-confidence grows. If he has learned to find rest inside the body of his wife, he feels sheltered just as a child does reposing on his mother's lap encircled by her arms. This physically experienced embrace by his wife's motherliness can help him to relax in his innermost being and can give him new strength, since he is so often attacked from outside, where often more is demanded from him than he can give. On the other hand, the wife who tends to lose herself in her subjective feelings will experience, in her husband's ability to master himself and wait for her, a strong fatherly hand to whom she can entrust herself. In this way she is able to let herself go completely because she knows that he will safely lead her through the turmoil of her emotions.

The greater the chance of the wife's coming to fulfillment, the less the husband's fear of being too quick or performing inadequately. The old adage "Nothing succeeds like success!" is very true here. It is up to the wife to give her husband confidence in his ability to love and thus to help him love himself as a man, just as he helps her to love herself as a woman.

Encircled and Sheltered

With this statement I have already pointed to the fact that the physical aspect alone is of no avail unless the *psychological* aspect is also brought into play.

I have intentionally begun with the body and not with the mind in my description of the sexual union, because this is biblical. The Bible starts with the body—creation —and ends with the body—resurrection.

When the Bible speaks about marriage, it says that husband and wife become one flesh. This term "one flesh" is used exclusively in the Bible in relation to marriage. It means, first of all, very concretely, the sexual union. But then it means even more. It means the whole person with body, mind, and spirit. It comprises the complete existence of the human being.

I mentioned already that for a woman body and spirit form a unity to a much greater degree than for a man. This is why women are considered more sensuous than men. Very often the husband does not understand the close relationship of both spheres, body and mind, for the wife. While he generally imagines that the mind is enveloped by the body, for her it is just the opposite: the realm of the mind envelops the realm of the body.

Dr. Bovet compares the love of the husband to a warm cloak. As long as the wife feels encircled, wrapped up in this cloak, she is able to surrender herself completely and unconditionally to her husband, both body and mind. In order to give her this feeling of being sheltered, the husband has to learn that it is not unmanly to express his feelings. If his words and caresses go together with the attitude of his heart, they will convey to her the message, "I am loved."

But even the slightest unkindness, a reproach, a harsh or inconsiderate word can cause a hole in the cloak and deprive her of the feeling of being sheltered and wrapped up in his love and thus make it impossible for her to surrender completely.

Silence does not mend holes. It is useless to try to heal a wounded heart by "having sex." The only way to mend it is to talk to each other and to share that which hurts.

If the husband makes an effort to mend the holes in the cloak through which the wind blows, the wife gains something which is essential for her ability to surrender, namely, confidence and basic trust. Just as the bird entrusts itself to the air when it flies and the fish to the water when it swims, so will she be able to entrust herself to her husband.

This ability to give herself completely is her deepest secret, but in order to be able to do this, she needs first of all to accept and love herself and be deeply thankful for being a woman. Simone de Beauvoir once said, "The goal of every woman is to forget herself—to give herself. But how can she do this if she doesn't yet know who she is?" This confidence in herself and complete trust in the sheltering love of her husband will enable her, figuratively speaking, to be able to jump off a cliff without any doubt in her heart that her husband will be there to catch her.

I remember watching our children learning how to dive. For the boys, it did not seem difficult to mount the high diving board, take a light jump, and then spring into the deep water below. When they had done it once, they were eager to try it over and over again. But for our eleven-year-old daughter, it was different. Each time she mounted the diving board, instead of running and jumping off, like her brothers, she hesitated and then in fear drew back. Her brothers kept encouraging her and urging her to try it, but it was only when her father dived in ahead of her and was ready to receive her in the water that she dared to do it, discovering in this way a new joy in her young life.

This is a good illustration of what the wife experiences in the act of love. She dives into the deep water without hesitation. She is not afraid, because she knows her loving husband is there waiting to receive her with open arms.

Coping with Sexual Frustration

"But what if you're all set to jump and your husband isn't there to catch you? What then?" a young soldier's wife once asked me, after I had spoken about this in a talk.

As a Christian, I believe the first answer lies in letting go and letting God. He can heal stress and it is possible to crawl up on his lap and be enfolded in his strong arms. It is possible to have confidence in him, just as a child has confidence in her father—to let yourself fall into God's arms. He will never fail you, for he keeps his promises: "Come to me . . . and I will give you rest" (Matthew 11:28). "Let him have all your worries and cares, for he is always thinking about you and watching everything that concerns you" (I Peter 5:7 *The Living Bible*). I love two words descriptive of our Heavenly Father which are often repeated in the Psalms: "steadfast love." Sexual frustration often leads to self-hatred. Only when we know that we are loved to God, can we again find that "basic trust" which enables us to love ourselves, and from this base to love and accept others.

We must face reality too and know that there are times when sexual satisfaction is impossible—when everything may be ready for fulfillment in the heart and body of a wife, but something interferes. Maybe the husband is involved in his work and this takes precedence. Maybe he's physically and mentally tired—we wives often forget that for a man intercourse diminishes strength and if a husband says he's tired, he probably means it. A French study has shown that the level of the male sex hormone testosterone is at its lowest level at 11:00 P.M. and at its highest level at 8:00 A.M. This too may explain a few things.

There may be times too when the husband is temporarily impotent. This usually is a psychological condition and is caused by fear and stress. Dr. Eric Berne speaks about this in a humorous way in his book *Sex in Human Loving:*

> Nearly all difficulties in erection originate with the operator and not with the mechanism—pilot's error, as they say in aircraft circles. The impulses to the penis are sent down from the brain and there is a little man up there who is supposed to keep his finger on the button when the signal flashes green and all systems are Go. But if he gets tired, scared, distracted, or upset, he may relax the pressure or release the button, even when the light is green. Since it is a fail-safe button or dead-man's throttle, once it is released, the mechanism is disconnected and goes back into idle. The little man is of course the Child in the person, and if he chickens out there is no erection even though all the wiring is sound and even though there is lots of stimulation coming in from the outside.[9]

It is a great help for the wife if she is able to share honestly her feelings with her husband, so that he is aware of them. If her fulfillment is temporarily postponed, then she must try to put this creative power into another channel. A hard physical task, like cleaning the basement or working in the garden, may help. Anne Lindbergh says that when she cannot write a poem, she bakes biscuits and feels just as pleased.

In *Markings*, Dag Hammarskjöld writes:

> Perhaps a great love is never returned. Had it been given warmth and shelter by its counterpart in the Other, perhaps it would have been hindered from ever growing to maturity.
>
> It "gives" us nothing. But in its world of loneliness it leads us up to summits with wide vistas—of insight.[10]

There will always be a last recess in our hearts which no human being can fill, for as St. Augustine has said, "God has created our hearts restless until they find their rest in Thee." Run into our Father's loving, everlasting arms and be covered by his steadfast love.

In many ways it is easier for a man to be satisfied sexually. He's thirsty, takes a drink of water, and then his thirst is quenched. A woman is thirsty too, but in the moment she is ready to take a drink, the glass falls and is broken into a thousand pieces—through a cross word, a disappointment—and she is left with her thirst. What then?

The temptation will come—perhaps another partner could satisfy her thirst better. Or perhaps she should masturbate and try to satisfy herself. This will often leave her with the taste of ashes in her mouth and an empty feeling. There is no bridge to the partner, no communion. Each partner becomes a fortress and the drawbridge over the moat between them has been drawn up. Dr. Seymour Fisher notes this recurring thought in a survey of all that has been studied about masturbation: "It encourages feelings of unreality by not only permitting retreat from the usual intimacy of the two-person sexual transaction but also by requiring the individual to split her identity by simultaneously playing two roles: the one who is delivering stimulation and also the one receiving it."[11]

A better way is for her to plan her day and include it in some of the simple joys of life. Even the Puritans said, "Outside of an healthy discipline, learn to be gentle with yourself." It's a lost day when we don't do something we really enjoy doing for at least half an hour. Self-pity is poisonous and will not lead out of the rut. It's no use crying over spilt milk, even if it may be precious nectar collected drop by drop. Look ahead. God is greater than our hearts and he has promised to wipe away every tear. Suffering makes us close to others and helps us understand them in their problems.

No one can *demand* love, for it is a precious gift. It is possible to give thanks each day for the little things and to learn for the future from our mistakes. To forgive and then forget—the best way to overcome a wrong is to forget it. To be resentful and have hard feelings will never bring fulfillment. Let us put our disappointments in God's hands. There are times when we may need to give up the ripe fruit of love into his hands—letting him use it to bear fruit for others.

How a Man Feels

A man desires to conquer his wife and to take her in his arms, while it is her greatest desire to be conquered by him and to surrender to him. But this act of conquering is only a chronological privilege of the husband. Once she is conquered by him, she in turn may conquer him and take over the initiative. The more mature a marriage is the more this reversal of roles will take place.

In order to understand this, it is important to know that the husband too needs the feeling of being sheltered. This feeling is conveyed to him if his wife makes an effort to understand him, to participate in the problems of his work, as if she were in his place. If she does this, she will always find something in his work which is worthy of praise which she can express to him. Few women realize how much a man is dependent upon the affirmation and acknowledgment of a woman. Nothing "conquers" him more than being praised by a woman. And if he receives more praise from another woman than from his wife, this may be the first step toward infidelity.

On the other hand, mockery and degrading criticism are poison for the male ego, which is often more vulnerable than the female ego. When criticism and failures have beaten him down all day, he comes home deflated, like a tire without air. Never does he long more for affirmation from his wife than in this moment. Through her praise she has to pump him into shape again. Marabell Morgan in her book, *The Total Woman*, has suggested that wives practice the four A's in their relationship to their husbands: Accept, Adapt, Admire and Appreciate.

He needs this kind of help also in respect to the physical union. Especially if he has not succeeded in bringing his wife to a complete fulfillment, he easily feels "guilty" and a "failure" and is afraid of the next time. Just then it is important that his wife, without false pretense, express thankfulness, that she say something positive and take the situation with a grain of humor. Degradation and criticism, however, would have a lethal effect. A liberated woman needs a liberated man. She never will be able to raise herself up by putting him down.

I know many women who never have experienced a total orgasm. Nevertheless, the sexual union is for them a joyful experience and they thank their husbands expressly for it.

Following ejaculation, the husband will have a feeling of satiation and even exhaustion. He has used up his physical strength. Therefore he has an irresistible desire to sleep. His wife must try to understand this.

On the other hand, the husband should understand that just as his wife needs a longer time to reach the sexual climax and just as she approaches it in a more gradual manner, so it is with her after orgasm. It's as though she has reached the top of a mountain, and on the summit has found a plateau. She likes to stay there as long as possible and is reluctant to descend. If her husband withdraws from her embrace, turns his back to her, and falls asleep immediately, maybe even snoring, then the magic—the wonder of this moment—is broken. It is as if a light goes out and the wife has a feeling of emptiness and quiet disappointment.

Her great need at this time is to be held by her husband, to feel his support and strength and to be reassured through caresses and words of his love for her. It is hard for the husband to feel into her need of hearing because he is afraid that the words may be devalued by repetition. But it is simply a fact: a wife cannot hear often enough that her husband loves her. Therefore not only caresses but words are of special importance, for strangely enough there is no other door through which the assurance of her husband's love can enter her heart than the ear. The heart, however, is her most sensitive erogenous zone.

In his *Handbook to Marriage*, Dr. Bovet has described the feeling between husband and wife at this moment as follows:

> After the storm of passion the two lovers are intimately opened up to each other, and can look straight into each other's souls. The happiness they have just experienced fills them with deep gratitude to each other and to God for giving them such a partner. They can now say and reveal to each other things which would not otherwise find expression,

problems are solved without saying a word, and they now experience what full communion can mean.[12]

May I briefly mention here that the quality of the experience of sexual satisfaction calls also for a bit of intelligence and good taste. All of us know the difference between quickly bolting down a hamburger and a malt, or dining leisurely in a romantic setting with candlelight. Hunger will be satisfied in both cases, and yet what a difference!

Love needs not only space, but also time. The unity of body and spirit cannot be achieved in a day. Love is like a small tree which can grow only if planted firmly into the ground of marriage. Like a tree, love is a living thing which cannot remain motionless. But it takes time for it to grow and to bring forth its choicest fruits, such as harmony in the sexual relation. Couples should not be discouraged if they have not found complete fulfillment during the first months or even the first years of marriage. Neither should they give up hope.

I remember when my husband and I consulted our marriage counselor once because of a problem we couldn't solve by ourselves. During the conversation I shed some tears. Then he asked us how long we had been married. I sobbed, "Eight years already." He smiled kindly and said, "You are still sucklings in marriage."

Then he told us that he and his wife had been married for forty-three years and that, as a medical doctor, he had studied marital problems and written many books about them during all those years. He added, "Now I believe I know just about enough to begin a marriage wisely."

Marriage is not a destination, but a journey. As husband and wife make this journey together, growing and maturing and learning how to love, they will reach sexual harmony as a ripe fruit of their marriage.

Praying with our Bodies

God accompanies us on this journey. He is present—always and everywhere—also in the physical union.

A Lutheran theologian, Dr. William Hulme, says:

> In the sexual relationship the realm of nature and the realm of the spirit coalesce—become united in Christian experience—because they first became united in Christ. . . . As redeemed by Christ, the sexual relationship is the God-given enjoyment of married love —for women as well as men. . . . The God whom we know in Christ does not have to be brought into sexual enjoyment—He is *there*.[13]

There are some couples who pray together every night except when they unite sexually. It is as if they had a bad conscience in experiencing sexual joy. They have separated their sexual life from their spiritual life. This separation, however, is entirely unbiblical. The God of the Bible, the Father of Jesus Christ who has become flesh, is the Lord of all realms of life, including the sexual realm.

In the fifth chapter of his epistle to the Ephesians, the apostle Paul testifies to the unity of the sexual realm and the spiritual realm in a way which is almost shocking to our ears. He says, ". . . and the two shall become one flesh. This is a great mystery, and I take it to mean Christ and the Church" (Ephesians 5:31-32).

Sexual joy can also have a positive effect on our spiritual lives. For couples who believe in God, the physical union becomes a spiritual experience. Because Christ is the center of their marriage, the act of love becomes a way of opening up to God in gratefulness. I know of no better words to express this more clearly than the prayer by Dr. and Mrs. Joseph Bird which is found in their book, *Love Is All: Conversations of a Husband and Wife with God!*:

> We made love last night
>   and today is new,
>   brand new and alive. . . .
> We made love and everything was re-created. . . .
> We talked,
>   we laughed,
>   and we prayed together with our bodies.
> And You were so very present.
>
> It's then that You always are,
>   especially then.
> Our closeness to each other
>   increases and makes more alive
>   our closeness to You. . . .
> And this morning?
>   This morning is sunrise,
>   and growing things,
>   and feelings of anticipation.
> Today is new, brand new and alive,
>   and the spiral of our love-making goes on,
>   drawing us together upward,
>   toward You.[14]

III

Living in Harmony with the Cycle and Fertility

The Blossoming of the Garden

"Mommy," said the eleven-year-old girl, "I have to tell you something." The mother was sitting at the bedside of her daughter and waiting to hear what she had to say. Finally it popped out. "I can hardly wait until I have my first ovulation." She was looking forward to it as if to her birthday.

Interestingly enough, the child did not talk about her first menstruation, but about her first ovulation. This shows that the mother had guided the talk with her child in the right direction. She had not stressed menstruation, but ovulation.

In this way she had given her daughter decisive help to accept herself later on as a woman. There's something mysterious about ovulation. I dare say that the knowledge of this mystery is indispensable if a woman succeeds in accepting herself. Not only will this knowledge help her to deal independently and responsibly with her fertility, but it will help her also to understand herself better in the ups and downs of her emotions.

A husband once asked me, "Why is my wife never the same two days in a row?" If he had taken the trouble to understand what happens to his wife in her body during the monthly cycle, he would know the answer. Therefore, it is important that not only women read this chapter, but also men.

Also for the single woman who wants to understand and accept herself, it is indispensable that she learn to live consciously with her cycle. Every woman should know what the eleven-year-old girl knew before her first ovulation.

In earlier times, people thought that the womb played the decisive role in a woman's cycle. They considered it the center of her being. The ancient Greeks believed that the moods of a woman originated in her uterus. The Greek word for uterus is *hysteros*, from which our word "hysterical" is derived. One considered the uterus as a garden, so to speak, and the days when a woman had her menstrual period were thought to be like the blossoming of the garden. Consequently one concluded that the days just before or after her period were her most fruitful days. The Africans see menstruation as a sort of "watering of the garden" and the opinion is widespread that in times as close as possible to this "rainy season," a woman is most likely to conceive a child.

We know now that this is not true. And yet, at the root of this unscientific idea there is a seed of truth. It is true that the time of blossoming, the time of rain, favors conception; but the time of "blossoming," the time of "rain" is not menstruation but ovulation. Not the uterus, but the ovaries have the decisive role in a woman's reproductive functions. It is only during the time of ovulation that she can conceive.

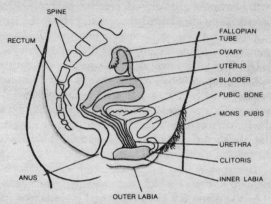

Fig. 4 Side view of the female reproductive organs.

Knowledge of the process of ovulation is the key if she wants to deal with her own fertility. It is just as indispensable for her self-awareness, self-acceptance, and self-love. Thus I would like to describe briefly what happens month by month in a woman's body.

The Orchestra Conductor

There is a small gland, called the pituitary gland, which is located in the head beneath the brain and behind the eyes. This little gland, dormant when the girl is small, is like an orchestra conductor who gives the signal for the music to begin. It produces certain hormones which in turn cause the sexual cycle of the girl to begin. The ovaries now begin to function and produce the hormones which cause the development of a girl's breasts, growth of the hips, pubic hair, and the other characteristics which physically transform a girl into a woman.

The ovaries are located one on either side of the uterus. They are almond shaped and about the size of a small plum. Near each ovary there is a passageway which leads to the womb, called the Fallopian tube.

Old Ethiopian medical books compare the design of a woman's reproductive organs with *la tête de boeuf*, the head of a bull. It is easy to see the resemblance. When my brother was teaching a class of 6th grade boys about the female reproductive system, he drew a diagram on the blackboard. One boy commented: "That looks like the head of a bull moose!"

The ovaries are filled with tiny eggs (more than 100,000 of them) which were already there at the time of birth. When the girl's menstrual cycle begins, one of these eggs gets ripe each cycle. Each egg (ovum) is very small—no bigger than the point of a pin and barely visible to the naked eye. Yet it is the largest cell in the human body. After an ovum is released from the ovary, it literally bursts into space and is picked up by the fingers of the open end of the tube which then leads it into the womb. If the ovum is not met by a sperm during its journey through the Fallopian tube, then the menstrual period will take place. As a famous doctor once said, "Menstruation is nothing more than the tears of a disappointed uterus." With the first day of menstrual bleeding, the cycle of ovulation begins all over again.

Hormones and Emotions

The two ovaries produce the sex hormones of the woman, of which there are two main ones, estrogen, which I would like to call here simply the hormone of femininity, and progesterone, which I would like to call the hormone of maternity.

As one sees in Fig. 5, there is a change in the balance

of both hormones during the cycle. The hormone of femininity (estrogen) is more active during the first part of the cycle and reaches its peak just at the time of ovulation. The maternity hormone (progesterone) is more active during the second part of the cycle. Progesterone helps prepare the lining of the uterus to receive a fertilized ovum. This explains also why a woman's temperature is at a higher level after ovulation than before ovulation. Progesterone also prepares the breasts to make milk, so that they are larger and more tender during these latter days of the cycle, just as they are during pregnancy.

A woman retains more fluid in her body and thus weighs a little more during the second part of her cycle when the maternity hormone has the upper hand.

A higher sensitivity level during the second part of the cycle and especially during the premenstrual days affects the woman not only physically, but also psychologically. Often she feels she can accomplish less during these days. She is more prone to become ill, she lives "heavier," is more easily discouraged and upset. The little difficulties of daily life may seem insurmountable to her. It is statistically proven that percentagewise, fewer women drivers are responsible for car accidents then men. But the women who do have accidents are more apt to have them during the days of premenstrual tension.

With the beginning of the next cycle, the femininity hormone, estrogen, again takes the upper hand and the woman begins to feel "normal"—feels that she is again herself. Her skin clears up, becomes more translucent. She is able to rise to the occasion, easily surmounting small difficulties, is happier and more optimistic. Women athletes reach their best and highest performance during this time. Even girl students do better in their exams during this part of their cycle.

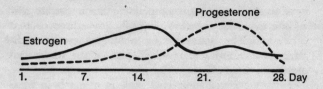

Fig. 5 Changes in ovarian hormones during course of cycle.
(See also Appendix B)

To accept yourself as a woman means to live consciously with your cycle: live with it and not against it! Therefore, self-awareness is an essential part of self-acceptance. This is just as essential for the single woman as for the married woman. The woman who is aware of her cycle is able to anticipate and then prepare. To know what causes difficulties reduces fear.

Even the daily schedule can be adjusted to the cycle to a certain degree. With a little bit of planning, one can avoid doing spring cleaning, having a large dinner party, or even moving just during the days of premenstrual tension. A husband who helps his wife to plan helps her at the same time to live in harmony with her cycle.

But this is possible only if he knows where she stands. Then he can understand also why she may be sad without reason, or irritated without an apparent cause. He knows that this is not a fault of character in his wife, but can be simply steered by her hormones. Thus he can see it all in the right perspective, which will help him to respond in the right way and not with biting irony: "That's just the way a woman is—incalculable and illogical." Instead it's the time for kind humor, a comforting word, or a good and understanding silence.

My husband claims that men also have something like a cycle and are prone more to certain moods at certain times. So far this cannot be proven, but it is a fact that men often react more to the cycle of their wives than they realize. Counselors and doctors who have to deal with men complaining about certain disturbances which recur periodically may discover that this is an unconscious reaction to the hormonally conditioned emotions of their wives—a reaction which can also affect the children.

This underlines once again just how much in marriage husband and wife are "one flesh" even to the extent of their emotions. Whether the changes in the hormonal condition of the woman are reflected in the intensity of her sexual desire is, however, an open question. It is a fact that a more intense desire during the time of ovulation—that is, during the fertile days—cannot be proven with scientific methods, even though this is maintained again and again. On the contrary, researchers in America and Holland point out that there is a greater desire in the days shortly before or just after menstruation.[1]

A French study done by the C.L.E.R. (Centre de Liaison des Équipes de Récherche) in Paris shows the same results. The time of *pleine jouissance* (complete sexual fulfillment) is experienced by the wife most frequently in the days preceding menstruation. Girls are often tempted to masturbate during this time.

What One Should Know about Ovulation

Here I come to a point which I purposely omitted in the last chapter: sexual joy can be considerably diminished by the fear of an unwanted pregnancy. In order to overcome this fear, it is important that a couple learn to deal with their fertility.

As Fig. 6 shows, the second part of the cycle is the same length for most women, approximately two weeks. It is a fact that this second part of the cycle, after ovulation has definitely taken place and after the temperature has been at a higher level for three days, is a cycle phase when a woman is infertile. Once ovulation has actually occurred there is no example in the medical literature of the world that a second ovulation has taken place, excepting the ovulation occurring within twenty-four hours after the first ovulation, which can result in the conception of fraternal twins.

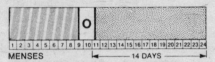

Short cycle of 24 days ovulation on day 10.

Average cycle of 28 days ovulation on day 14.

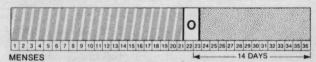

Long cycle of 36 days ovulation on day 22.

Fig. 6 POSSIBLE CYCLES OF ONE WOMAN: When the cycle varies in length, it is the pre-ovulatory phase that becomes shorter or longer; the post-ovulatory phase remains constant.

The first part of the cycle varies in length from cycle to cycle and from woman to woman. Most women have, depending upon the length of their cycle, some infertile days also during the first part of their cycle.

It is possible to determine the time of ovulation.

There are certain symptoms or signs which indicate it. Ovulation usually occurs just before the rise of temperature. The higher temperature level indicates that progesterone, the maternity hormone, now has the upper hand. Another indication that ovulation is taking place is the greater amount of cervical mucus.

The determination of the time of ovulation is not to be confused with the Rhythm or Calendar Method, let alone with the so-called ten-day rule. These methods rely upon a probability calculation and are unreliable because the length of the cycle varies and is unpredictable.

The method I want to propose is entirely different. It does not rely upon arithmetic, with a greater or less probability, but is an exact observation of symptoms which are independent from the length of the cycle. This method is called the Sympto-thermal Method. But before I describe it, I would like to relate how my husband and I learned about it.

Help for the Bush

As I have mentioned already, we lived for several years in Africa (Cameroun) among a very poor population. A flooded river isolated our station from the outside world for six months each year. The next doctor and the next hospital were almost two hundred miles away.

The problem of conception regulation came up for two reasons. On the one hand, we found an unexpectedly high number of childless couples. This was the result not only of sterility from venereal diseases, but also of the traditional wrong biological information about fertile days. For these couples we sought a way in which those days could be determined with greater certainty. On the other hand, the necessity of limiting the number of children becomes a more and more pressing issue in Africa today. One reason is because the education which African parents want to give their children is very expensive.

Therefore we looked for a method of conception control which met the following conditions: (a) it had to be reliable; (b) it should be inexpensive; (c) the application should not involve any health risks; (d) no doctor's help or supervision should be necessary; (e) it should be applicable and accessible for every couple, even in the remote African bush.

None of the methods we knew at that time met those conditions. In addition to that, we had the following difficulty. Africans in general have an instinctive aversion to all artificial means of conception control—whether they be of mechanical or of chemical nature. Many African governments are very skeptical and distrustful of these methods. This was illustrated by the action taken at the United Nations World Population Conference in August 1974. In many African states, family planning by artificial methods is forbidden.

After our return to Europe, we kept looking for a solution. In an issue about contraception in an Austrian medical journal, we read an article by Dr. Josef Roetzer. From his address we saw that he lived only a few miles from our home.

The guidance of God is often unique and unexpected. Our encounter with Dr. Arnold Kegel in Los Angeles, as reported in the previous chapter, was such a unique guidance. Our encounter with Dr. Roetzer was a similarly unique experience. Just as Dr. Kegel had made his life's work the research and study of the pubococcygeus muscle, so had Dr. Roetzer worked for two decades on how to determine scientifically the fertile days of the woman. He had examined tens of thousands of female cycles. Much of that which I pass on in this chapter, I owe to collaboration with him.

The more we become acquainted with the results of his research, the more we recognized that the method which he proposed met precisely all the conditions that we needed for our work in Africa. Not only was it reliable, demanding neither money nor doctors, not only did it cope with the African's aversion to artificial methods and was no stumbling block for any government—it was also easy to apply, even for an illiterate population. On our lecture tours in Africa, we realized very soon that the observation of the cervical mucus was in general nothing new for African women. Many of them were aware of these symptoms, but they were ignorant as to their meaning in relationship to their fertility.

In addition, this method had a side-effect which helped to reach one of our main goals in Family Life work in Africa: it favored the dialogue between husband and wife.

Help for the Bush Only?

When talking to couples in Europe and America, we discovered that many were ill at ease with the methods offered to them in dealing with their fertility. Here too we met a certain hesitation and reluctance—and this not only from Catholic couples.

No real solution has been found yet in America and Europe, as shown by the growing number of abortions. If the proposed methods of conception control were as safe and as satisfying in their application as is often claimed, the problem of unwanted pregnancies should actually no longer exist.

Lack of discipline as well as lack of information also plays a role here.

Dr. Roetzer says, "Chemical or mechanical methods

are not one hundred per cent reliable except during the infertile days of the cycle." (And then they are unnecessary anyway.)

For many couples they evidently are not satisfying either, because they are emotionally disturbing. These couples have the choice between either sacrificing the joy of a sexual union or risking an unwanted pregnancy.

Therefore, we believe that this method is an answer not only for the countries of the Third World, but also for America and Europe. The knowledge of it is spreading rapidly throughout the world. I shall describe it briefly here.

Description of the Sympto-thermal Method

The Sympto-thermal Method relies upon two scientifically proven facts: (a) during the time of ovulation certain physical symptoms can be observed; (b) after ovulation has occurred, the basal body temperature rises.

A conception can take place only when a certain mucuslike fluid is produced in the cervix (the neck of the uterus). During most of the days of the menstrual cycle, the mouth of the uterus is blocked by a mucous plug, preventing the sperm from penetrating into the uterus. When the time of ovulation approaches, the cervix opens wider and becomes softer. The mucous plug becomes thin and more fluid. There is so much of this mucus produced that it pours out like a small waterfall from the cervix into the vagina. This causes a condition which is favorable to the life of the sperm. This mucus enables the sperm to move quickly from the vagina, penetrate the cervical canal, and move into the uterus.

Ovulation can be recognized by five symptoms:

1. A feeling of wetness at the mouth of the vagina is often the first symptom of approaching ovulation. Most women experience a slight discharge on all days of their

cycle, but this differs in that it is more profuse. As the day of ovulation approaches, this discharge from the vagina becomes more clear, sometimes even transparent, similar to raw egg white. If a woman examines it on a Kleenex or on a piece of toilet paper, she will notice that it is wet, slippery, and stretches without breaking. The German medical term is *Spinnbarkeit* (that which can be drawn into a thread).

Just as every woman recognizes the days when she has her menstrual period, so it is possible for a healthy woman to learn to recognize the days just before and during ovulation when she has this cervical mucus. The cervical mucus is not a sign of sickness, as some women fear—even asking their doctors about it; its purpose is actually to receive the husband's sperm and to help them in making the trip to the wife's uterus and tube. It should be noted here, though, that the use of vaginal sprays and douches can hinder the observation of the cervical mucus. Their use is discouraged by most gynecologists anyway.

2. Another symptom or sign of ovulation which many women recognize is a sharp pain in their lower abdomen, usually on one side or the other, like a knife jab. This is the so-called *Mittelschmerz*, or midpain, and is felt in connection with the congestion of the ovary as it is ready to ovulate. In one cycle this midpain may be felt on the left side and in the cycle following on the right side. While having lunch recently with a young couple who were both competent in fertility awareness and who knew how to recognize these symptoms, I noticed the wife wince as she took her place at the table. Her husband winked at me and said, "That's her midpain." He was very well informed about the symptoms of ovulation, although he was not a doctor but a technical engineer.

3. Some women notice a small amount of pinkish

blood or "spotting" at the mouth of the vagina during these days. This is probably due to the drop in estrogen after the peak level causing ovulation, which in turn causes small quantities of blood from the uterine walls to mix with the vaginal secretions. I have talked with young women who confuse this symptom with menstrual bleeding and think they have especially irregular cycles.

4. Some women notice that on the days just before ovulation they feel a prickling, tingling sensation in their breasts which can be distinguished from a heaviness and soreness which occurs as a premenstrual symptom.

5. In order to be very sure and to have an additional proof, one can also measure the waking temperature. *After ovulation has occurred* there is a rise in the level of the woman's basal body temperature which remains until the end of the cycle. The change in the temperature is due to the secretion of the hormone, progesterone, which also prevents the release of another ovum from the ovary. Progesterone is secreted by the corpus luteum, which is formed in the ovary after ovulation. A stable high-level temperature thus indicates conclusively that ovulation took place on one of the days before the rise in temperature.

One can take the temperature with a normal fever thermometer. The thermometer should be shaken down the evening before and be at hand on the bedside table. *Immediately* after waking, the temperature should be measured for five minutes, either rectally, vaginally, or orally. The French take it vaginally, the Germans rectally, and the English orally. So take your choice. Each one is effective. To measure the temperature under the armpit is unreliable. The rectal measurement is the most reliable.

Each day the waking temperature should be recorded as shown in Fig. 7. Between menstruation and ovulation the temperature will stay at a lower level. Then it rises sometimes abruptly but mostly over a period of two to four days by 0.4 to 0.6 degree Fahrenheit or even higher. It remains at this level for about twelve days, then drops just before the next menstruation begins. If conception has taken place, the temperature will remain at the higher level. If this higher temperature is recorded for more than nineteen days, it indicates that the woman is pregnant.

In order to have a reliable measurement of the waking temperature, it is necessary that the woman have at least one hour of rest before taking it. This means that even if a mother has to get up several times during the night because of a sick child, she can still take her waking temperature effectively. Even women who work on night shifts and have to sleep during the day can take their waking temperature. All that counts is that the temperature is taken approximately at the same time of day after the woman has had at least an hour of rest. If the woman has a fever, the temperature will rise sharply so that the difference from a normal temperature-rise after ovulation can easily be recognized.

Many women object to this method, thinking it to be of no use because they have very irregular cycles. But that means that they have not yet understood the main point. It is especially useful in the case of an irregular cycle, because it relies on symptoms which occur regardless of the length of the cycle. In addition to that, the method can help a couple to understand why, in spite of their desire to have a child, the woman does not get pregnant. If the temperature stays at a low level from one menstruation until the next menstruation, this can be a sign that no ovulation has taken place during this cycle. If the high temperature plateau is too short—less than seven days—the fertilized ovum cannot nest in the uterine lining and is expelled at menstruation. In both cases, treatment is possible.

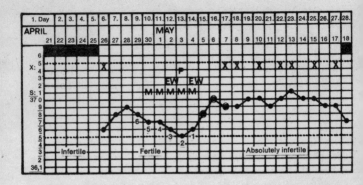

Fig. 7 Days 1-6 are infertile; the thick border line between day 6 and 7 indicates this. The three consecutive higher temperature points are marked by drawing a little circle around them. Preceding the circles, the days counting back from 1 to 6 indicate the six preceding lower temperature points.

M = mucus   EW = mucus looking like egg-white (stretchy)

P = mid pain   X = intercourse (without contraceptives)

If a couple make a temperature graph as shown in Fig. 7, they can easily determine the fertile days. A clinical temperature chart, as used in hospitals, is worthless for recording the waking temperature.

After ovulation, the ovum has a life span at the most of twenty-four hours when it can be fertilized. The sperm of the husband lives longer; however, it is able to fertilize the ovum for only one or two days. Therefore, according to the rule that Dr. Roetzer has formulated after years of study and experience with thousands of couples, the time in which a child can be conceived is limited in general to the six days before the rise of the

temperature and the first two days of the three consecutive higher measurements *after* the mucus symptom has
ceased. These three measurements can be called the
"three hot points" and are encircled in Fig. 7. The evening of the third "hot point" belongs already to the absolutely infertile time. Because the survival of the sperm
is dependent upon the length of the mucus phase, conception may occur in rare cases even earlier than six days
before the rise. On the other hand it may also happen
that the fertile phase begins no earlier than three days
before the rise of the temperature. The combination of
the observation of the cervical mucus which helps to recognize in advance the approach of ovulation, plus the
observation of the temperature rise, offers the highest
possible certainty of determining fertility and infertility.

Advantages

1. *Help for self-acceptance:* In the first chapter I
pointed out how important it is to accept yourself in
order to love yourself as a woman and how the acceptance of the body is an integral part of this self-
acceptance. The self-awareness and self-observation for
which the Sympto-thermal Method trains us is a tre-
mendous help for this physical self-acceptance. Therefore a young girl, whether she plans to marry in the
near future or not, should start to live consciously in
harmony with her cycle and become aware of her emotions and physical symptoms.

2. *Deepening of the one-flesh union:* For the married
woman this method can add a new dimension to the
experience of oneness with her husband, for it forces
the couple to talk together. It presupposes that a dialogue is established and maintained. It is inapplicable

unless the husband participates in the physical experiences of his wife, and loves her as his own body (cf. Ephesians 5:8).

A new respect for the partner as one of God's creations, and therefore a new respect for each other as a person is gained. It is not that either one or the other adopts an "object" or a "thing," but as a couple they begin a new way of life. Practically speaking, this means that the husband may now and then take care of the children while his wife takes her waking temperature.

The periodical abstinence from intercourse is not experienced as a loss, but as an asset. A French couple has expressed it this way: "It has helped us to play on other registers of love and to discover other forms of bearing fruit."

Those who speak in a mocking way of "love according to schedule" have never experienced this dimension of being one flesh, especially since it cannot be proven that the wife is more longing on the fertile days. If this should be the case, perhaps it has psychological rather than biological reasons—comparable to the experience of good Roman Catholics who in times when they were supposed to abstain from eating meat on Fridays, had every Friday a special appetite for meat.

Here again the testimony of a couple is: "Just because the periodical abstinence takes effort, it has added to our love a new quality and protected us from monotony. . . . When we wanted a child and therefore had intercourse more frequently, the experience became not quite as fulfilling. In times when we don't need the discipline, as for instance during the time of pregnancy where there is neither menstruation or ovulation, it is almost as if something is lacking."

The feeling to be desired in times when a sexual union is not possible gives the woman a sense of gratefulness and self-esteem. At the same time the respect which she feels for her husband grows, because he gladly renounces the sexual union for the sake of love. An American couple told us recently that when they were asked by a group of young couples whether it wasn't difficult to abstain certain days each month, the husband said: "On the contrary, it's like having a period of courtship and then a honeymoon every month. It keeps our love fresh." This common discipline sheds a new light on the counsel of the apostle Paul to couples: "Honor Christ by submitting to each other" (Ephesians 5:21, LIVING BIBLE).

3. *Fertility awareness:* The Sympto-thermal Method makes it possible to plan for a child when one feels guided by God to do so instead of leaving it to chance.

Once a very devout German pastor's wife expressed her conviction to me that she thought the Calendar or Rhythm Method was the only method allowed for Christians, just because it was so unreliable and in this way gave God at least still a chance. She mixed up God and hazard. We are not exposed to the powers of hazard, like a ball to be tossed back and forth, but we are children of the Heavenly Father, guided by his Spirit (cf. Romans 8:14).

Between 10 and 15 percent of all couples are childless. Often the desire for a child has to remain unfulfilled. One reason is because the husband is infertile. But in many cases such childless couples can be helped if one knows the time most favorable for conception. Sometimes this may be only a few hours during the cycle of the wife, but it is usually not longer than four days for any woman, depending on the length of the mucus symptom.

It is rather late to begin to study one's fertility pattern after the first baby is born. The young girl who has learned fertility awareness long before marriage will bring this knowledge as a definite contribution to her married life.

On the other hand, a conception can never be forced.

For even on the fertile days there is still a probability of 40 percent that conception will not take place. It is not something which we can manipulate. Fertility awareness is certainly no manipulation of God.

In this day of smaller families, many couples may want to plan the sex of their child. The sex of the child is determined by the father who has two types of sperm —those called X and those called Y. The X sperm cells produce girls and the Y sperm cells, boys. The sex of the baby is determined at the moment of conception depending upon whether an X sperm or a Y sperm has reached and penetrated the egg first. Recently doctors have made the interesting discovery that the two types of sperm have actually different shapes. The male-producing sperm are round-headed and smaller; there are many more of them and they are able to travel faster. The female-producing sperm are larger, oval-shaped and seem to live longer. This means that a couple who has intercourse before the egg is released are more apt to have a daughter than if they have intercourse just at the time of ovulation when the egg has already left the ovary and is waiting to be fertilized. The boy sperm swim faster, get to the tube sooner and will thus fertilize the egg if it is there. If it is not yet there, they die and the longer living X (girl) sperm are there to meet the egg. If a couple wishes to have a son, they could plan intercourse on the day of ovulation or shortly after. This may be a help for some couples.

One mother who identified herself as not being affiliated with any religious group wrote as follows:

> The reason that I am greatly enthused about natural family planning, and will use it to the exclusion of any artificial method of contraception, is not because of religious or moral reasons, but because of health reasons. Artificial contraception is yet another way

of pollution. It pollutes the body just as our city water and air, the many additives in our foods and bottle-feeding do. You are aware of the fact that with the ecology movement more and more people are becoming interested in antipolluting ways of living in every form possible. Birth control will be no exception. Let's hope that eventually natural family planning will be used by all those interested in keeping themselves, and the future generations, as pure as possible.[2]

4. *The independence of the couple:* The couple become independent not from God, but from their doctor. Most effective contraceptive measures, above all the so-called pill, demand medical supervision and prescription. But the question is: why should a healthy and normal woman be forced to become a patient when she wants to deal with her fertility?

The Sympto-thermal Method enables the couple to become their own authorities and to become independent from the doctor when dealing with their fertility. This method helps them to preserve their dignity as human beings.

A word has to be added here explaining why so many doctors are ignorant or skeptical of this method. This is actually not their fault because, although many of the biological facts mentioned above were taught when they studied and were mentioned in their medical textbooks, no application was made to family planning. Therefore, when a friend of mine who had observed the cervical mucus asked her gynecologist about it, all she got for an answer was: "It's nothing to worry about." She received as little information as those women in the African bush.

Marriage and the problems connected with it are not yet in the focus of most medical training. Often a doctor gives a prescription without sufficiently considering the effect it may have on the marriage relationship as a whole and not just on the patient as an individual. An example of this is a new type of neurosis causing problems of impotence, which Christa Meves, a leading German psychologist, attributes to "the pilled woman." Such a wife may over-demand her husband sexually.

Another question which the reader may have: is the Sympto-thermal Method reliable enough to rule out any fear of an unwanted pregnancy? Reliability could be added here as a fifth advantage. I prefer to answer this important question in detail and would like to present here a comparison between this natural method and artificial methods.

Artificial Methods

Dr. Christopher Tietze of New York, an internationally known expert in the field of family planning, in his latest reports divides the theoretical effectiveness of different methods of contraception into four groups: (1) most effective methods; (2) highly effective methods; (3) moderately effective methods; (4) least effective methods.

In the first group of the most effective methods the pill appears. The only other method mentioned in this group is the method based on the strict application of the waking temperature. If one adds to this the observation of the cervical mucus, then the use-effectiveness is even greater than that of the pill.

If one can imagine that one hundred couples apply one of the following contraceptive methods for one year, they have to reckon with the following number of unwanted pregnancies. (If no means of contraception whatsoever is applied, there is a minimum chance of sixty of these hundred women getting pregnant.)

USE-EFFECTIVENESS OF
CONTRACEPTIVE METHODS[3]

The figures represent the number of unwanted
pregnancies per 100 woman-years.

METHOD	FAILURE RATE
Coitus interruptus (withdrawal)	10–38
Vaginal douche	21–36
Diaphragm with cream	4–36
Cream or jelly alone	7–42
Condom	6–19
Calendar	6–14
Intra-uterine device	3–5
Temperature alone	0.5–1.3
Sympto-thermal	–0.7
Pill	0.7–1

Often the possibility of failure is not mentioned when
one of these methods is recommended to a couple. Dr.
Roetzer writes the following:

> None of these methods succeed in preventing con-
> ception with absolute certainty. . . . The cause of this
> unreliability lies in the nature of the few fertile days
> of the woman. Naturally during those few fertile
> days, the most favorable conditions exist for the
> sperm to find their way from the vagina through the
> uterus to the ovum. Even with the technical achieve-
> ments of the second half of the 20th century a
> method has not yet been invented which provides an
> unsurmountable hindrance for the sperm. This
> means that the knowledge about the fertile days is of
> importance for all couples, regardless of which
> method of contraception they use. During the few

fertile days they are to a great extent doomed to failure.[4]

That the method of withdrawal, or interrupted intercourse, and also the application of a condom diminishes the joy of the act of love is evident. The high failure rate of the condom is especially striking. The reason is that even if it doesn't tear, some sperm may escape at the upper edge during intercourse. There is also the danger of losing it after the erection recedes.

I.U.D.s (intra-uterine devices), which are inserted into the uterus to prevent the nesting of the fertilized ovum (which means they hinder the development of an already conceived living being and therefore are abortifacient), are foreign bodies in this sensitive organ. They may cause a chronic inflammation of the endometrium (lining of the uterus), and not all women are able to tolerate them. I.U.D.s also cause augmented menstrual bleeding. Besides that, there is a danger that the I.U.D. may be lost without its being noticed. For some time many thought that I.U.D.s would be the answer for the countries of the Third World, for example in India. Indian women who suffered from chronic anemia, however, lost too much blood during menstruation when using the I.U.D. making it a health risk.

Even the sterilization of the woman is no absolute protection. Complications as a result of this operation cannot be excluded. After it has been done, many women are unable to cope with it psychologically. Here is a typical quotation from a mother of two children, in her thirties, which may speak for many: "One year ago our second child was born. Right after the birth I had my tubes tied. I just can't cope with this fact and find no inner peace. Even though I hadn't believed this possible, I experience it as a heavy burden."

Many may think that a vasectomy for the husband

would be the answer to all fertility problems. The fact that there are three million vasectomized men in the United States is a sign of this trend. The initial operation is much simpler than a tubal ligation for the wife. Here are some facts which should be considered by couples contemplating this step:

First of all, it is never a solution to basic marriage problems. If a couple can't talk to each other and there's a lack of understanding on the part of both, this will not solve their problems of communication. Only a husband who has a healthy self-image and self-identity is able to undergo this operation without damage to his personality.

Also, 6 to 10 percent of vasectomized men in the United States ask for a reversal of the operation because of divorce and remarriage. But this is not a simple procedure.

"Our marriage was good before, but I'm never quite sure now if I can trust my husband to be faithful to me," army wives, whose husbands were vasectomized during their stay in Vietnam, have told me time and again. I believe as John and Nancy Ball have said in their unpublished paper, "Conjugal Love and Conscious Parenthood": "Rather than eliminating their fertility, a couple should live in awareness of their fertility. . . . We do not question the motives or sincerity of married couples who may have taken such measures. Few of these couples ever felt they had any real alternative."

Now a word about the pill which contains estrogen and progestagens. These are synthetic hormones produced in the laboratory and resembling the natural hormones secreted by the ovary during the cycle. They prevent the release of an ovum, providing the dosage is high enough, thus imitating artificially a state of pregnancy. If one knows the meaning of ovulation for the entire female organism, it is not surprising that many women are affected psychologically. They complain of stomach troubles, vomiting, headaches, but also about frigidity, depression, and irritation.

If one tries to diminish these unwanted side-effects by a different composition of the pill, one diminishes at the same time its reliability. Another factor which lowers the reliability is that many women simply forget to take it. If this happens only a few days, ovulation can take place and conception can occur. After discontinuing the pill, the return of menses may be retarded or delayed. It may take several months or even years before the cycle has readjusted to its natural rhythm. When this does not happen, a complicated medical treatment which is not always effective may be necessary in order to establish the menstrual periods. Dr. Roetzer calls the pill "a biological atomic bomb." A girl who is using the pill should check with her doctor about possible complications.

Dr. Rudolf Vollman, an American gynecologist, has spent a lifetime researching the menstrual cycle. His findings are soon to be published under the title of *From Menarche to Menopause,* Biostatistics of Women's Reproductive Physiology (W. B. Saunders & Co., Philadelphia). He likens the cycle to the finger print of a woman, and says that using the pill is like putting a woman's reproductive organs in a strait jacket. It is the first time medicine is being used to damage a physiological process to such an extent.

Concerning the long term effects of the pill, I would like to quote from Dr. Roetzer's book:

One question which has not yet completely been clarified is the possible damage to posterity. The oldest children of those mothers who took the pill for a longer period of time before they conceived are now between 15 and 18 years of age. So far no malformations have been observed. However, during recent years one has noticed augmented hereditary damages when examining the abortive material of those women who previously had taken the pill. It is a question here of spontaneous abortion (miscarriage) of unviable embryos which were damaged in their hereditary substance. This gives at least a hint that the pill may affect this substance. Geneticists call our attention to the fact of the possibility of a hidden hereditary damage of children who seem outwardly healthy. Children who have been conceived after their mother took the pill for a longer period of time may have altered or imperfect genes. The marriage of two such bearers could have a catastropic effect. Therefore in any case, the prescription of the pill, especially for young women who have not yet had the number of children they wish, should be handled with great reservation. At least the time of prescription should be limited and only considered as a temporary solution.

According to the present state of scientific knowledge, it is irresponsible to prescribe the pill for the same patient over a number of years.[5]

For the woman during premenopause and after, when pregnancy is not recommendable and therefore no damage to posterity is possible, the prescription of the pill has to be considered from a different point of view. But for a woman who may be twenty-six and who has all the children she wants and with about twenty fertile years ahead of her, the pill is no long-term solution.

Here I would like to add a word for young girls. I can only warn them against taking the pill, because it disturbs their whole physical development. Yes, they may even remain permanently infertile. After taking the pill for a longer period of time, the "withdrawal" bleeding can cease completely and a complicated treatment may become necessary.

There seems to be a connection between the availability of the pill and the sex-consumption of our time. The alarming increase of venereal diseases through promiscuity—that is, through the constant change of the sexual partner—is certainly related to the use of the pill. There is no protection against infection as was provided, for instance, through the condom.

If one keeps all these observations in mind, one cannot help but conclude that the application of artificial methods *en masse* always backfires. The reason is that evidently artificial methods do not correspond to the nature of the human being as a creation of God. The body which has been created according to certain laws rebels. The natural means of conception control correspond more to the dignity of the human being. "Nature bats last."

Therefore, it is important that experts who have worldwide experience of teaching natural methods meet and share their views. I would like to report about such a conference.

An International Symposium

An International Symposium on Natural Family Planning was convened by the Human Life Foundation in Washington, D.C., in June 1973, with travel expenses underwritten by United States AID. The delegates came from Canada, North and South America, Australia, Korea, Taiwan, India, Indonesia, and the Philippines. Representatives also came from France, Austria, Holland, and Italy. From their meeting a new organization came into being which is now called International Federation for the Promotion of Family Life. (See the Basic Principles in Appendix.)

My husband and I took part together with Dr. Roetzer. What impressed us most at this conference, besides the deep spiritual atmosphere, was the fact that most participants came as couples and passed on their experiences together. The Drs. François and Michèle Guy, from France, told about their experiences with illiterates during their stay on the Mauritian Islands.

Drs. John and Evelyn Billings, from Australia, have developed the method of self-observation of cervical mucus to such a degree that they believe it no longer necessary to take the temperature in order to determine the time of ovulation. Many participants considered this a potential breakthrough, with special promise for application to Third World nations because of the simplicity of the method. The Drs. Billings speak of "wet days" when the woman is fertile and "dry days" when she is not. Dr. Roetzer doubts, however, that this simplification of the method is as applicable, for instance, in Austria and Germany, because the ability of healthy self-awareness in the so-called developed countries is still underdeveloped.

The best-organized and most widespread organization is SERENA in Canada, run by a group of couples. (SERENA stands for the French "Service de Regulations des Naissances.) This organization has trained more than 250 teacher-couples who visit other couples and pass on the method by way of personal testimony. According to the principle, a couple teach couples. They have informed more than 150,000 people. To me this opens also a new way of marriage counseling for the future.

What became very clear to us during this symposium was the fact that Natural Family Planning is not simply an approach to contraception with greater advantages or disadvantages. It offers actually a new way of life, because it is based on a different image of man.

a new way of life, because it is based on a different image of man.

Manipulation or Education

There is a tendency in our technical age to try to bring everything under human control, so that it can be "made" and manipulated. The illusion prevails that it would be sufficient if one would only make the right object available to man in order to enable him to solve his deepest problems—as, for example, a condom, an I.U.D., or a pill. At first glance there seems to be a certain success, but the backfiring which all the "thing" methods have caused, especially in the underdeveloped countries, shows that the way of the technological short-cut will fail in the long run. Abortion as a means of birth control is the last consequence of this belief in human manipulation. When man is not recognized as a creature of God, the liquidation of human life is the logical consequence.

Of course, it is much simpler and much less time consuming for a doctor to take the technological short-cut and to prescribe a "thing" rather than to educate a couple. However, the question is: does he serve their marriage as a whole? Does he serve their humanness?

Natural Family Planning proposes a way of self-education. True, it is the longer way and requires more effort, at least while it is being learned, but it is also the more rewarding way. It helps a marriage to graduate from the kindergarten stage and makes it possible for a couple to live in harmony with the rhythm of fertility which the Creator has given the woman. It takes account of the fact that one of the differences between man and animals is that man has no time when he is "in heat," but that he is able to make a free and responsible decision about his fertility. This freedom of choice is essential for the humanness of man. Natural Family Planning corresponds to the biblical image of man.

I close this chapter with the personal testimony of a French couple:

> What shall we say after ten years of marriage? The Sympto-thermal Method has given us a way of life which has made our love grow. The periodic abstinence is possible only out of love and makes love deepen at the same time. The self-awareness and the self-acceptance serve the developing of the personality. Fantastic, to be able to call a child into being, when the right moment has come!
>
> . . . We are convinced that God has put a meaning into human sexuality which lets us stand in awe before the greatness of the human being. Even if we do not feel this awe all the time and if many may never feel it, we believe that it is profoundly true. The Sympto-thermal Method helps us to practice day by day the respect before the miracle of the creation of the human being.[6]

IV
The Wonderful Time
of Expecting

Certainty

> Pregnancy is very much like making love.
> Only in carrying him and his love within me,
>   the union of our sexual love lasts longer.
> It's as if the heights of our love-making
>   continue on in richness
>   and fulfillment
>   for a full nine months.[1]

There are some women who may be shocked or in violent disagreement with this statement. But I know others, and I include myself among them, who echo it in their hearts. The miracle and deep happiness of carrying new life, and the sense of unity with one's husband, defy description. My own mother once told me that she wept bitterly when she realized that her years of childbearing were over.

Again I have to think here of my African sisters. They feel best, and love themselves as women most,

64

when they are pregnant. Then it is easiest for them to accept themselves.

The joy of anticipation of a child starts with the certainty that one is pregnant. The earlier one has this certainty, the longer will be the joy of anticipation. Those who apply what was described in the previous chapter are able to have this certainty at the earliest possible time.

Please compare the three cycles of the three women recorded in Fig. 8 (p. 66). Mrs. B wanted a child and planned it, and now she can immediately be certain that she is pregnant. Once this certainty is reached, there is no greater joy for the future mother than to share it with her husband.

Shared Joy—Shared Responsibility

I would like to dedicate this chapter especially to husbands who love their wives enough to try to understand what they experience during the time of pregnancy.

In the Sistine Chapel in Rome, Michelangelo has painted "The Creation." He depicts God the Father reaching out his right hand to touch the finger of Adam and give him life. The Creator's strong left arm is encircling Eve, the mother of all the living, just as if to say, "This is my helper, my co-worker in the mystery of creation." When a husband looks at his pregnant wife and thinks of her as God's co-worker in the task of creation, he will have a new respect for her. He will stand beside her to protect and help her in the work of bringing forth new life.

Dr. Margaret Liley, from New Zealand, writes in her book *Modern Motherhood*: "Pregnancy is a shared responsibility and one of the most inter-dependent conditions of life. The woman can no more get through her

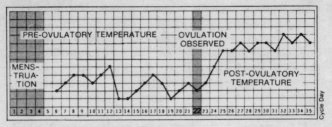

Mrs. "A" expects her menstruation on day 37. Mrs. "A" knew she ovulated around day 22 from her temperature chart. She did not have sexual intercourse on her fertile days.

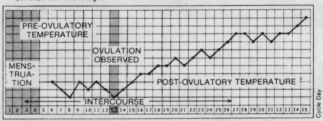

Mrs. "B" knows she is pregnant. Mrs. "B" observed her ovulation on day 13. Her temperature remained at a high level in the post-ovulatory phase for more than 20 days.

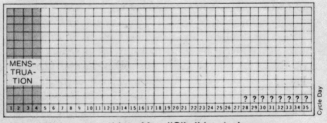

Mrs. "C" knows nothing. Mrs. "C" did not observe her ovulation. She does not know if she is pregnant or if her cycle is unusually long.

Fig. 8 Case of 3 women who have not menstruated by the 35th day and whose cycles usually vary between 27 and 33 days.

pregnancy successfully without the man, than the baby can get along without her."[2]

Pregnancy unites husband and wife in a new way. Their child is one of the greatest fulfillments and fruits of their marital love.

When a woman knows that she is to become a mother, she is filled with awe. Mary, the mother of Jesus, replied to the angel who told her she would bear a son: "Behold, I am the handmaid of the Lord. Let it be to me according to your word" (Luke 1:38, RSV).

The deeper the wife feels this awe and wonder, and expresses it to her husband, the more he too will sense it. This will help him to take over his part of the responsibility and to love himself as a father.

A father can do nothing better for his child than to love the mother of his child. This statement is valid not only after the child is born and during the growing-up years, but especially during the time of pregnancy.

How Life Begins

The life of a baby begins with one single cell, smaller than the period at the end of this sentence. This cell is created by the union of the female egg cell or ovum and the male sperm cell.

The female egg is light yellow and round like a ball. Normally only one egg ripens each month, in one of the two ovaries of the mother. This ripe egg bursts out of the ovary (some women feel a knifelike jab in their lower abdomen when this happens) and falls into the trumpet-shaped opening of a hollow tube (called the Fallopian tube), which is about 4 inches long. The inside of the tube is no larger than a hair bristle. There are two tubes, one leading from each ovary to the mother's womb, the uterus. The tiny egg cannot move by itself, but is drawn into the Fallopian tubes by ciliary cells which, along with muscle contractions, carry it on toward the uterus, much like the ciliary cells of the nose carry mucus toward the back of the nose. The egg can live only a short time—from twelve to twenty-four hours. Unless it meets a sperm during this time, it soon dies and about two weeks later the woman begins her menstrual period.

The male cells are produced in the testicles of the father. They are much smaller than the ovum—2,500 of them would just cover the period at the end of this sentence. Under the microscope, the sperm cells look very much like tadpoles, because each one has a head and a tail, and can swim. One can travel the 7-inch distance through the uterus into the tube in an hour. The sperm can live only from twenty-four to forty-eight hours after leaving the testicle and being deposited at the mouth of the uterus. It will remain alive and fertile only if the cervical mucus favoring it is present. Otherwise, it will die within a very short time.

God is very generous in his creation. As many as 500 million sperm cells are ejaculated at the time of intercourse. Only one of these millions will be able to reach the ovum and fertilize it. The walls of the uterus, with its folds of tissue, are like high mountains for the tiny sperm, and in climbing each mountain, many sperm cells are lost. Only the strongest are still alive when they reach the tubes.

As soon as they are near the egg, they become excited; their tails lash about more rapidly and they race to see which one will get there first. That one pushes its head forward to penetrate the protective covering of the egg. Once the sperm cell has entered, no other can penetrate. It now pushes ahead to reach the center of the egg. There it joins with the female cell and these two lie side by side, and are completely united. Here lies the deepest mystery of the one-flesh union. Within this half hour of union, traits of the new baby are decided within the tiny egg—whether it will be a boy or a girl, short or tall,

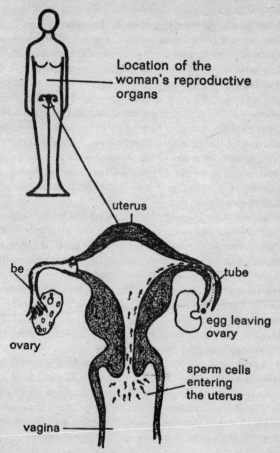

Location of the woman's reproductive organs

uterus

be

tube

ovary

egg leaving ovary

sperm cells entering the uterus

vagina

Fig. 9 The moment of conception when the egg and sperm cell meet in the tube.

whether it will resemble more the father or the mother. Each new baby is a unique individual, never entirely like either parent or any ancestor.

Three hours later, the egg begins to divide into more

cells. As it moves toward the uterus, it continues to develop within its original skin. It remains free in the uterus for five or six days, but then all its food is used up, and it must make a nest if it will survive. All this time, the walls of the uterus have been growing softer and fuller, and the egg now makes a nest for itself in this soft bed. The ovary produces the hormone progesterone, which is the great friend of the egg because it does two things: (1) It prevents the uterus from contracting at the time it normally would for the menstrual period, and thus expel the egg. (2) It also keeps any other eggs from developing in the ovaries during the months of pregnancy. That is why there is no ovulation during pregnancy.

About once in eighty births, twins are born. There are two reasons for twins growing in the mother's womb. Either the egg which has been fertilized divides into two separate parts, which means that two babies start to grow instead of one, or two separate eggs are released at the time of ovulation and both of these are fertilized by two different sperm cells. Twins from a single egg are always the same sex, and are called identical twins. Fraternal twins from separate eggs are no more alike than other brothers and sisters.

About one time out of five, an egg that is fertilized is defective, and the uterus will empty it out. Such miscarriages, "spontaneous abortions," happen most often in the second or third month of pregnancy. It is not the fault of either the father or the mother, and the chances are that the next pregnancy will be quite normal.

The First Months of Pregnancy

This is the period of adjustment—mother to baby, and baby to mother. Her whole system can be upset. Often she is very sleepy and thus needs more rest than usual. She may be nervous, irritable, and cry without reason.

What she needs from her husband during this time is nothing more, but also nothing less, than simple understanding. He must understand that these reactions are not moodiness or lack of self-control, but are biologically conditioned. If her husband says to her that he understands her, and does not reproach her, this will be a deep comfort for her. She will find it easier also to accept herself in this new stage of her life.

Often the first physical sign of pregnancy for her will be a prickly sensation in her breasts. They also become somewhat larger, and she may notice a white, cakey substance on the nipples. This is called colostrum, and comes as a preparation for the time when she will nurse her baby.

She will also notice that she must urinate more frequently. This is because the growing uterus puts pressure on the bladder. The uterus, in its normal state, is about the size of two large thumbs held together. At the end of three months of pregnancy, it has grown to the size of two fists held together.

The greatest difficulty for an expectant mother during this period is to know how to deal with the nausea which she may feel, especially when she gets up in the morning. This is because she has not eaten for several hours, while her baby has taken nourishment constantly from her body, thereby causing her to have lower blood sugar. She can find relief if she avoids letting her stomach become completely empty. She should not eat much but, rather, small amounts of food more often. Her husband could be a big help, simply by bringing her a cup of sweetened tea and zwieback or toast in the morning, before she gets out of bed. Psychological factors can also play a role in morning sickness. It is the time when the mother needs to be mothered herself.

Sometimes, she develops an appetite for strange foods during these first months. A wise husband should not react to her wishes with ironic remarks, but should try to satisfy them, even if it costs him effort and money. Nothing can win the love of his wife more than when he shows her by such little things that he is concerned about her well-being. This is, of course, true at all times, but especially so when she is carrying his child. These months will soon pass, and then she will carry good memories in her heart of how her husband has shown his love to her. Good memories cost time and effort and sometimes even money.

It is not true that an expectant mother must eat for two, but in order for her to have a healthy pregnancy, she must drink for two. She does this for several reasons. One is that more fluid is lost from her body because she breathes more rapidly. (The air breathed out is filled with moisture, thus causing a fluid loss in the body.) Too, a woman usually feels warmer in pregnancy, because her baby is like a little heating system. Therefore, she perspires more, which also causes a fluid loss, especially in hot weather.

A very important reason why doctors advise an expectant mother to drink from six to eight glasses of water daily is because it helps the mother to carry off her own waste matter, plus the baby's. If this is neglected, the waste may accumulate in the mother's body, and both her health and that of the baby will be in danger. Physiological processes which happen in the body of the mother also affect her baby.

After the first month, the "embryo" (meaning "little bud"), as the baby is now called, is ¼ inch long. Already its heart has started to beat, and it will continue to beat until death.

At the end of two months, the baby's face is formed, as well as arm and leg buds with the beginnings of fingers and toes. The backbone has also begun to form. The tiny egg has now grown to be the size of a small hen's egg, and the baby itself is an inch long.

At three months, the teeth are already forming, and it may be possible to identify the baby's sex. The unborn child is no longer referred to as an embryo, but as a fetus. It is this boy or this girl who is killed in case of an abortion. The mother is also definitely affected by an abortion. As a wise woman told me: "It is like picking a green apple. When you do that, a piece of the tree goes along with it."

The Nice Middle Months of Pregnancy

These are the most pleasant months—a time of acceptance and harmony for mother and baby. Mothers usually feel wonderful during this time. They begin making plans for their baby. Between the fourth and the fifth months, the mother will feel the first butterflylike movements of her baby. Just as muscles grow in an athlete's body, so the muscles of the uterus keep increasing in size, growing new tissues with stretchier fibers as the baby grows.

By the end of the fourth month, the fetus is from 4 to 6 inches long, and weighs ½ pound. This is the time of the most rapid growth.

At the end of the fifth month, the baby has doubled its weight, and is from 8 to 10 inches long, weighing about a pound. The heartbeat can now easily be heard. The eyebrows and eyelashes are growing, as well as the hair. Muscles are developing too.

It is important that the expectant mother watch her posture carefully. Here too her husband can be helpful. He should take notice that she stands correctly. She should walk like a queen, with her shoulders pulled high rather than back. If he praises her in her efforts, and addresses her lovingly as "Queen" or "Her Majesty," this may be an incentive for her to work on her posture.

If, however, the expectant mother has poor posture, her whole body is thrown out of balance, because the weight on her frame is in the wrong place. It may help her to think of her baby as an egg in a shell in an upright position, and to carry it that way. African women can do this better than their American and European sisters, because they know the secret of balancing weight on their heads. This is impossible to do if they do not walk uprightly.

When a woman picks up something from the ground or reaches down to a small child, she should always squat down, keeping a straight back and bent legs. If she bends over and thus puts a great strain on her back, she will certainly have a backache at the end of the day.

There is one exercise an expectant mother should do every evening before she goes to bed. She should get down on her knees on a small rug, placing the palms of her hands on the floor. In this position, she humps her back like a cat, and lowers her head. Then she makes a hollow in her back while she raises her head. This she repeats about twenty times while breathing regularly. The husband should take over the counting, and not allow her to get into bed until she has done this exercise, which will relieve her of backache, help prevent varicose veins, and improve her general well-being.

There is a proverb which says that the mother grows more beautiful with each child she bears. This is especially true if she feels loved by her husband, who is proud of her appearance and finds her attractive, not only as a wife, but also as a mother.

There is nothing wrong with having intercourse during pregnancy. It cannot harm the baby. The baby grows inside a balloonlike sack, called the bag of waters. This is filled with a salty fluid which protects the baby

a) Hump back like
camel, lower head

b) Make back hollow,
raise head

Fig. 10 How to do pelvic rock exercise to relieve backache.

Wrong way

Causes backache
and strain

Right way

Notice straight
back and bent knees

Fig. 11 How to bend down.

from shock and from temperature changes. Even if the
mother falls down or is hit, the baby will rarely be hurt.
An additional protection is the mucus plug which closes
the cervix and hinders germs from entering the uterus.

In case a woman has had several miscarriages, it is well to abstain from intercourse on those days when she normally would have had her period, during the first three months of pregnancy. But in general one might say that everything which makes the mother happy during pregnancy is also good for the baby. During the nice middle months, the mother is most relaxed, and therefore very open to all signs of love, and especially the sexual union. This can be due to the increased sensitivity of the vagina and the lips around it.

That's why if she says she longs for love and tenderness, she means it, and her husband should understand. After all, he is the father of her child, and she would like to show him her gratefulness in this way.

The husband too goes through a process of change during his wife's pregnancy. He senses the growing responsibility. Sometimes people joke that it is easier to *become* a father than to *be* a father, but I think that both are equally difficult. The feeling of being left out may bother him a lot and make it difficult for him to master the task of self-acceptance as an expectant father. No wife should forget this.

The Last Three Months of Pregnancy

For a mother, this is one of the most exciting periods of her life. It's hard for her to sleep, to think straight, and often her feelings will overflow to her husband. After nine months of carrying her baby, she is full of expectation, knowing that soon she will see her child.

During the seventh month, the baby opens its eyes. It has a wrinkled look and is large and strong enough to be able to live outside its mother's body.

During the eighth month, the baby becomes more beautiful, because a layer of fat is developing under its skin, taking away the wrinkled look. Between the seventh and the eighth months, the baby rotates so that its head is down. It actually stands on its head before it is born. Sometimes this does not happen (about six times in 100), and then the baby is born with the buttocks first (breech birth).

During the last month of pregnancy, the baby settles low in the pelvis, which again causes the mother to have to urinate more frequently. She may also suffer from constipation. Sometimes she feels her baby having hiccups.

The mother's body is now preparing for labor, as the muscular tissues in the cervix, vagina, and pelvic floor soften and become more stretchable. Often she feels her uterus becoming hard, and the muscles contracting. These are called "Braxton-Hicks contractions," and are like practice labor which prepares the uterus for the actual birth.

An expectant mother's diet should be balanced with plenty of protein, fresh fruits, and vegetables. An egg a day is the golden nugget of nutrition. Her urine and blood should be examined regularly, especially during the last weeks of pregnancy.

When a child is ready to be born, it will come. The average pregnancy, if you count from the first day of the last menstrual period, will last 280 days. For example, if a wife had her last period beginning February 15, then she would count ahead nine months, and add seven days, which would be November 22. It is very normal, however, for a baby to be born up to two weeks earlier than this date, or two weeks later. This can have something to do with the date of conception in relation to the length of the menstrual cycle and the time of ovulation.

The time of waiting can deepen the relationship of the expectant parents tremendously. It is a rich and fulfilling time. The following prayer, written by an African mother, expresses this in a very beautiful way.

Loving heavenly Father, almighty and everlasting
God, Creator of us all:

Thank You for the joy of knowing that a new person
is growing within me;

Thank You for using me in Your work of creation.

Keep me and the child safe during these months of
waiting.

I think of Jesus, born just as my child will be born:

Help my child to grow up like Jesus, strong and wise
and loving, and knowing You as his heavenly
Father;

Help me, like Mary, to put myself, my husband, and
my children into Your hands,

With complete trust that You will do what is best
for us all.

V

Birth—A Marital Experience

Listening to the Mothers

The physician of the Dutch royal family was asked what he thought about the father being present at the time of birth. He gave the surprised answer: "Where else should the father be at that time?"

Indeed, where else? I have always felt a little sorry for men because they can never know the joy of giving birth to a baby themselves. It is all the more important, therefore, that the father participate as much as possible, so that the birth may become a marital experience.

When a baby comes into the world, a father is born with him. Nothing can help the husband more to grow into his fatherhood and accept it than to have a role to play in preparing for birth, and also at birth itself. Nothing can help his wife more to accept her motherhood than the participation of her husband in this experience. Now she learns to love herself not only as a woman, but also as a mother.

But who listens to us mothers? Our opinions about the treatment and care of the mother during birth are not asked in our society. Administrators and specialists who have never felt the quickening of new life themselves make decisions above our heads. They figure out with their minds how hospitals should be built, and which rules and policies should prevail. The realm of feeling counts but little to them, while it is a decisive factor for a new mother. That special gift of mothers, a sensitivity for physical and psychological needs of others, is suppressed and therefore changes into feelings of inferiority and insecurity. The rules invented by hospital administrators are often hostile to mothers, with the result that the birth experience does not strengthen marriage and family life, but on the contrary weakens it. Mothers treated unjustly, who feel themselves "reduced to nothing," as one mother put it, transfer their feelings of anger and disappointment to their husbands and children.

Overruling this deepest need of a mother is discrimination against the mother, which I believe is a direct result of the discrimination against women in our society today. The emancipation of the woman includes the emancipation of the mother. As the liberated man belongs to the liberated woman, just so the liberated father belongs to the liberated mother. And the liberated father, if at all possible, should be present at the birth of his children!

The Liberated Husband as Father

In a lecture which Prof. Dr. Niles Newton gave before the American Medical Association in 1972, she said the following:

Medical rules also usually forbid a father to see the birth of his own child, and to give emotional support to his wife in the later parts of labour, in spite of the fact that the medical team is often so rushed that it does not give friendly conversations to the labouring women.

Birth is a psychological crisis. While experiencing crisis the human being has a special propensity for forming strong attachments to those around them. When the husband is excluded from participation during labour and delivery, many women appear to form intense attachments to their obstetricians instead.[1]

The well-known American obstetrician Dr. Robert Bradley, who has delivered more than eight thousand babies in the presence of their fathers, confirms this. He reports that it happened to him again and again, that mothers after a successful delivery, wanted to embrace him in spontaneous joy. And he adds, "I would be embarrassed at such moments if the husband were not there."

In tradition-bound Africa, this suggestion may be still more unusual than for us. And yet I found a surprising openness with African men to this idea. When I talked recently to African theological students about this topic, one of them said: "Certainly I agree with you. We would like to be present when our wives give birth. But the old women who take care of them during delivery do not permit it. They claim that this is a unique privilege of the women, and men have no business in being there."

Is this reaction only typically African? Can we not also find it in America? Sometimes I sense a feeling of insensitivity, even hostility toward husbands on the part of nurses, midwives, and obstetricians. I wonder what is behind this feeling. Is it envy or the desire to dominate the scene, as in Africa? Or is it simply the desire to get a job done in the most efficient way possible? Or, to state it differently, is it the desire to block the husband's way to liberation?

Here is the report of a woman whose husband had received the permission of the doctor to be present at birth:

> Tony received a white coat and was allowed to join me in the delivery room. But after some minutes, he was called out again and had to give up his coat, because the head nurse did not tolerate his presence. All we could do was to wait for the doctor. Tony prayed outside, and I prayed inside that permission would be given. When the doctor came, Tony got his coat back again and was allowed to enter the delivery room. It was a very great joy for him to see his son being born. But afterwards, the head nurse threatened to resign unless it was specifically stated in the rules of the hospital that no husbands would be allowed in the delivery room in the future.

Of course, I realize that such a position is motivated not only by hostility and stubbornness. Outward circumstances often make the presence of the father impossible—as, for example, in countries where hospitals have more than one delivery taking place in the same room at the same time. The underlying question here is, "Why were hospitals built that way in the first place?"

If the husband is forced to leave his wife in the lurch during this decisive hour, it may become very difficult for him to accept himself as a father. This conflict is shown in the following letter written to me by a Bavarian farmer:

> After my wife had been in labor for some time, I brought her to the hospital and stayed with her until it was time to go to the delivery room. Then the nurse said to me in a commanding voice, "Now the

husband goes home." Which I obediently did. But I felt so miserable, so base, such a coward. I was ashamed of myself and felt like I had betrayed my wife. But then I thought, there's nothing which can be done about it.

Here's the report of another couple, where the husband insisted on being present. His wife writes:

No one seemed to care what was going on in my head—all they were interested in was the physical progress going on at the birth end. Only my husband asked me about my feelings, and this was a precious gift. He kept me informed about how far along I was, talked to me, and encouraged me. What was happening to me brought us very close together, because it concerned both of us. And then the joy when our baby was born! Of course, the doctor and nurses congratulated me, but what was that in comparison to the joy expressed in the glowing eyes of my own husband?! We had brought our son together into the world. I purposely say "together" because through the help of my husband, I had much less pain. To experience these first moments after the birth, together, is magnificent, glorious! Birth—not to be left alone in labor; the baby—not to be left alone in joy. This binds our family closely together. It was wonderful to know that there was someone who was praying for me, very specifically, because he was aware about what was happening. I just can't imagine childbirth without my husband—except as a terrible aloneness.

Here is how her husband described the experience in a letter to me:

Seated at my wife's head, I could follow the process of birth. The first movements and the first cry of our baby gave me indescribable joy. Now it is clear to me why you urged us to experience the birth together. It was indeed a mountaintop experience in our marriage.

Ten minutes in labor can be a long time for a woman! I would have felt like a criminal if I had left my wife alone in these hours. It was important for me to be there to wipe the perspiration from her brow, and whisper comforting words into her ear. She held my hand, and knew that I prayed for her. We talked about everything under the sun. Every time a contraction came, I reminded her of how to breathe correctly, as we had practiced it, and also I helped her to relax between the contractions. Prenatal exercises are not only the concern of the wife, but also of the husband; at least he must be informed about the physiological and technical aspects of them.

My presence at the birth was not only meaningful to me, but it helped my wife at the same time to be distracted from pain and to concentrate on the coming baby. I just can't understand why a husband should be excluded from this experience.

Many doctors seem to underestimate this psychological side of the birth process and the husband's role in it.

After all, the husband has promised to be his wife's closest confidant—to help her and protect her always. How can he leave her alone then during this crisis? A wife who feels forsaken here is easily inclined to become hostile to her husband. This new entity, husband-wife-child, can only become a reality if the husband can accompany his wife in all stages of her becoming a mother, and his becoming a father. Of course, I believe that he has to be well-instructed about the process of birth with all its side effects. I am very thankful here for Dr. Bradley's book, *Husband-Coached Childbirth*.

Guide and Coach

Yes, he must be instructed, or rather, *both* must be instructed. A birth is like a journey which husband and wife undertake together into an unknown country. Together they study the route they are going to take. The more the husband is informed about everything which is ahead of her, the better he can be her guide through the unknown country of birth.

Dr. Bradley says that the husband should be a sort of coach or trainer, because the trip will demand great effort. He likens childbirth to an athletic event. If an athlete is to do his best when playing a game, he must be trained. A mother, too, must be trained for childbirth, and the husband is the best trainer. Of course, if he wants to be a trainer, he must know which muscles have to be strengthened, which exercises are needed in order to help his wife to give birth with as little pain as possible, and in this way reach the goal of the trip. Therefore he tries to understand the difficulties which his wife will have to face during certain stretches of the journey and help her to overcome them. He is not an additional bother to the doctor, but a necessary ally and a go-between for his wife and her birth helpers.

Dr. Pierre Vellay, a world-renowned French gynecologist, who delivers over a hundred babies each month, told me that he prefers only those women as patients whose husbands are willing to participate in a childbirth training course. When I told Dr. Vellay that other doctors tell me that they have no time to teach the husbands also, he answered simply: "I have no time *not* to instruct them, because the length of the birth process can be an hour to an hour and one half shorter when a prepared husband and wife work together to deliver their child."

As Sheila Kitzinger, an English sociologist and childbirth educator, says in her excellent book *Giving Birth*:

The husband is usually the best person to give labor support, even though a good many start off with qualms about their role. He more than anybody else, usually understands his wife's responses (and if he does not, maybe this is a good time to learn). He knows when tension is building up before it is apparent to anyone else, knows how to soothe and calm her, and the right words with which to give her new confidence and courage. . . .

When a husband is present during labor, it is most important that he has a constructive and necessary part to play, and is not simply a "hanger-on" and "voyeur" on the scene of labor. He needs to feel that he has a definite task to perform, and should never be put in the position of being a mere observer.[2]

I would now like to help husband and wife get acquainted with the travel route of this journey together. They should know it well in advance so that the birth of their child can really become a happy and dignified experience for both of them. Dr. Vellay often says, "It is the woman's hour of greatest dignity." Ignorance and uncertainty make a wife tense and fearful. However, if she knows what is ahead of her, she can overcome fear. Her husband can encourage her and strengthen the powers of her will, so that she can look forward with happy anticipation to a good birth. It is the right of every child to have a good birth, especially since this gives him the greatest chance not only for survival, but also for a healthy life.

It may be well to realize that God doesn't always will a fruitful, happy ending and sometimes he plans a different route than we think. If he does, the expectant parents may experience an entirely different form of blessing, unity and growing. Especially if there are serious problems with the baby the mother needs the love

and support of her husband even more. My brother
writes: "I've seen many difficult, complicated deliveries,
premature births etc. which have drawn parents closer
together in a way which is inspiring to behold."

The Goal of the Journey—Childbirth without Pain

Really? Is it possible not to have pain during childbirth? I have met devout women who claimed in all
sincerity that it would be something like a sin to try to
avoid pain during birth. Does the Bible not say, "In
pain you shall bring forth children?" Isn't the woman
trying to flee from the curse put on her if she tries to
avoid pain?

First of all, God did not curse the woman. He cursed
the snake (cf. Genesis 3:14), and the soil (cf. Genesis
3:17), but he did not curse Eve or Adam. The Hebrew
word which is often translated "pain" really means
"toil," "labor," "hard work," and is the same word
which is used in reference to Adam in Genesis 3:17. "In
toil" Eve shall bring forth her children, and "in toil"
Adam shall bring forth the fruits of the earth all the
days of his life. To bring forth children in toil does not
necessarily mean great physical pain. It only points out
that the birth will take great physical effort.

For me, the person of Eve is overshadowed by the
person of Mary, who says simply when the angel an-
nounces to her that she will be the mother of Jesus:
"Behold, I am the handmaid of the Lord. Let it be to
me according to your word" (Luke 1:38). In these
words, which express her complete surrender to God,
Mary does not deny the difficulties ahead of her, but
they are overshadowed by the joy of expectation, so that
Mary sings a song of praise (cf. Luke 1:46–53).

Jesus himself points out the strange combination of

suffering and happiness: "When a woman is in travail, she has sorrow because her hour is come; but when she is delivered of the child, she no longer remembers the anguish [literally translated 'pressure'; to be in a narrow place], for joy that a child is born into the world" (John 16:21).

For this reason, I believe that a mother can look forward to a birth with joy. Bringing forth new life, which relates her closely to the Creator, can be both a happy spiritual experience and a happy physical experience, giving her a new dignity and self-acceptance.

The First Stage of the Climb

In order to be able to experience childbirth as much as possible without pain and fear, two things have to be learned and practiced: the right way to breathe and the right way to relax. Labor is strenuous. It is like climbing a mountain. There are some parts of the climb which are easy. Other parts are very steep. At all times, it is necessary that the body has enough oxygen. This is especially important for the unborn child. Oxygen is indispensable for life, for it carries away the poison in the blood. Without oxygen, the cells in the body die. The brain especially needs a great amount of oxygen.

Therefore, the right way of breathing is of great importance during labor. Before labor starts, during all the months of pregnancy, the expectant mother should make a practice of breathing deeply and slowly.

Her husband can help her learn how to breathe correctly by counting to three while she inhales slowly through her nose. Then she should hold her breath for one second. After that, she exhales slowly through the nose while he counts, "One, two, three." This exercise should be repeated several times until it can be done without effort. The time of inhaling and exhaling should

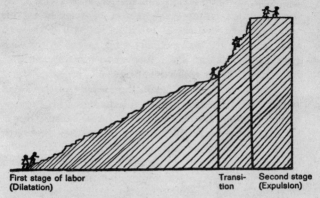

First stage of labor
(Dilatation)

Transi-
tion

Second stage
(Expulsion)

Fig. 12 Childbirth like climbing a mountain.

be gradually prolonged until she is able to breathe in for ten seconds, hold her breath for four seconds, and again breathe out for ten seconds.

Once the mother-to-be has learned the art of deep breathing, it can be adapted to the different lengths of contractions, as you see in Fig. 14.

Relaxation too has to be practiced. This can be done as follows:

The wife should lie down on a rug with a small cushion under her head and another one under her bent-up knees. (The legs should not be stretched out flat because this can cause cramps.) Her shoulders should be back, elbows pointed away from her body, hands open. First of all, she should relax the muscles of her face, then neck, arms, abdominal muscles, buttocks, legs, and feet—first tightening them one at a time and then letting them go.

After the wife has done this, she remains relaxed, breathing softly and regularly. She says to herself: "I'm completely relaxed." Her husband should raise her right arm, and let it flop down, then her left arm. Twice a day for about ten minutes she relaxes consciously in this way, so that when she is in labor, she will do it with ease between the contractions of her uterus. After each period of relaxation, she rolls over to her side and gets up slowly so as not to become dizzy.

I would like to stress again the exercise of the Kegel muscle, mentioned in the second chapter. This exercise is just as important before as after birth, because this is the muscle strand which opens and closes the birth canal, as well as the urinary and rectal openings. She can practice drawing up on it just as she would do to stop the flow of urine, drawing in her navel at the same time and then counting slowly to three. Slowly, slowly she lets the muscles go until they are completely slack.

Sheila Kitzinger proposes that the mother-to-be think of the Kegel muscle as an elevator in her body, which she pulls up to the fifth floor. Little by little all the muscles are tightened . . . first floor . . . second . . . third . . . still higher . . . fourth . . . fifth. Now stop! Try to go one story higher! Hold it for a few seconds! Now go down slowly.

The mother should practice this twelve to twenty times in a row at least twice a day. She can do it in bed before she gets up in the morning, or when sitting or even standing. It is a great help in preparing the muscles of the pelvic floor for childbirth, as well as in aiding them to return to their normal shape after childbirth.

When the mother feels a slight backache together with contractions in her uterus, she knows that birth is imminent. At first she may feel the contractions every half hour, and they may last only thirty seconds. But gradually, they will become more frequent and last longer. The time has now come for her to prepare to go to the hospital. The mountain climb begins now in earnest. She knows that it may be a very stiff climb, for which she needs all her strength. At this moment she can put herself into the hands of her Heavenly Father, and pray as this African mother has prayed:

The Lord is my Shepherd
    Therefore I lack nothing. . . .
Loving Lord,
Be near me now.
    Take away my fears.
Give me strength and patience.
    Help me trust in Your perfect love and care.
Give wisdom to my helpers,
Give life to my child, and joy to us all.

                                        Amen.

Uphill

The time of walking on a relatively level plain has passed now. The path becomes steeper. The climb uphill should not begin with shallow breathing and tenseness. The mother needs to put into practice now all that she has learned about deep chest breathing and relaxation. Everything that distracts or hinders her from concentrating on the goal ahead should be avoided.

What happens in the mother's body during this uphill climb? It may help to think of the bottom part of the uterus as a funnel. Before the baby is ready to be born, the neck of the uterus, the cervix, is long and narrow and closed with the mucus plug. When the baby is ready to be born, the upper part of the uterus, which consists of very strong muscles, begins to contract.

Every time the womb contracts like this, the head of the baby is pressed down on the narrow passage at the bottom. This is the longest stage of labor and is called dilatation, which means opening. It is usually longer for a mother giving birth to her first child (it may last a whole day), than for a mother who has already given birth. (See Fig. 13.)

During this stage the mother may notice some thick mucus lightly stained with blood, at the vulva. This is

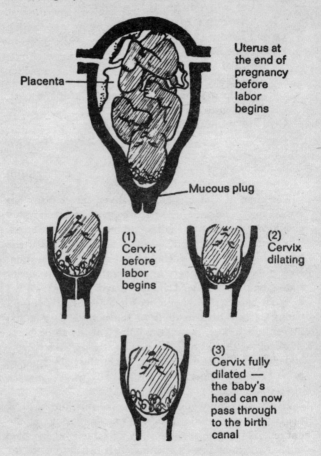

Fig. 13 How cervix changes during first stage of labor.

called "show." When she sees this sign she knows that the passage is beginning to open up.

As long as the contractions which cause the cervix to dilate are weak, lasting only a few seconds and felt only every ten to fifteen minutes, the mother can still walk around and even do light work. But as the contractions come closer together, she will want to rest. Now the deep breathing is very important. Each contraction is like an ocean wave. At the beginning of the contraction, as she feels the uterus hardening, the mother should take a deep breath, hold it a second, and then breathe out—the so-called cleansing breath. Then she takes another deep breath and breathes lightly until the contraction is passed. It will look something like this (see Fig. 14).

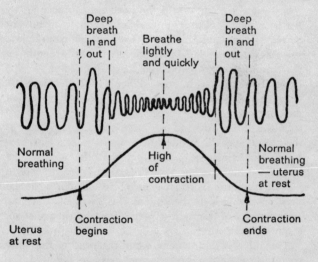

Fig. 14 How to adapt breathing to contractions during first stage of labor.

This way she learns how to ride on the crest of the wave without being pulled under by it. When the contraction is finished, she takes another deep breath and then breathes out deeply as she returns to normal breathing. By doing this, the mother can climb uphill for a long time without getting too tired.

Often toward the end of this stage, the bag of waters will break. This is called the "rupture of the membrane." When this happens, either a lot of fluid comes out suddenly or it seeps out a little at a time.

It's high time now to be at the planned place of delivery. Cleanliness is important at this stage, because after the rupture of the membrane, germs can penetrate the uterus, and the danger of infection is greater.

Steep Ascent

It is now a great help if the husband can accompany his wife during this climb and tell her how to breathe correctly. He should take care that between contractions she relaxes completely and conserves her strength for the transition period which comes at the end of the first stage. Transition is the most difficult time of childbirth. Even though it is usually quite short, it is the steepest part of the climb. Here especially she needs the encouragement of her husband, for often she will lose heart at this point and think that she cannot go on. Her husband's objectiveness, telling her that the goal is just ahead and that she has already accomplished the stiffest part of the climb, is of great help. He tells her what she may not be able to believe at this moment, that the steepest part of the path is very brief, and then she can push the baby out.

Transition is the moment when the head of the baby passes through the very narrow passage between the backbone and the pubic bone in front, from the uterus into the birth canal. It is the most uncomfortable time of labor, but the goal is just ahead. Often the mother's body trembles and she does not want to be distracted. Faster deep breathing helps relieve pain. However, it is not yet the time to push. The mother would just be wasting her energy, for the baby's head has not yet reached the birth door. This would be as foolish as driving a car out of the garage when the door is still shut. It was a help to me during transition to think of the baby, and that soon I would be holding it in my arms. My sister Veda, who had delivered hundreds of babies as a nurse in Tanzania, and who was present at the birth of one of our sons, said, "It's the shortest, but most dangerous, safari of his whole life."

Plateau

The steepest part of the mountain is now past. Just before the summit there is a plateau. The mother has now begun the second stage of the birth, namely, that of expulsion. If her husband tells her, "You have the most difficult stretch behind you now," she will stop being anxious that she can't make it and this will give her comfort and new strength for the next decisive contractions.

The Last Climb to the Summit

These contractions come very often now, nearly every minute. If the membrane has not ruptured before, it will do so now, and the head will appear. Each time a contraction begins, the mother must take a deep breath, breathe out, another deep breath, and hold it while she pushes. She knows now instinctively that it is time to push, for the baby is ready to be born and it would be difficult not to push. Actually, the contractions of the uterus are chasing the baby out, and the mother does this pushing almost hilariously.

It often happens that this is the moment when the obstetrician does an episiotomy. It can easily happen that through this operation, the Kegel muscle is hurt, especially if a medio-lateral incision is improperly made, which could lead to sexual inadequacy. Concerning this practice of episiotomy, Dr. Niles Newton, herself the wife of an obstetrician, asks the following question:

> Why do we routinely cut so many women at the end of the second stage of labor as the baby descends the birth canal? Tears can usually be avoided if women are correctly positioned with legs not spread too wide apart and when they push in a controlled manner following instructions. In many other countries, with favourable maternal child health statistics, labor is managed in this way to avoid both tears and episiotomies in all but a few women. An intact perineum is a matter of obstetrical pride and I am sure a great comfort to mothers who don't have painful stitches. I do not know of a single well controlled scientific study showing health advantages in cutting the woman's perineum as delivery approaches in normal labor. I wonder whether this custom is not part of a basic philosophic assumption that "faster is always better."[3]

The Peak Experience

The mother can feel the baby sliding out, but it is not painful. It is important now that she pants, taking short little breaths, in order to avoid pushing as the head and shoulders slide gently out. It is the couple's greatest hour as they see their love blending into a new individual.

This joy can even be a sexual experience, provided that the mother is not under deep sedatives.

In her book *Natural Childbirth and the Family*, Helen Wessel quotes the following account of a mother who gave birth to a nine-pound child:

> . . . it was ecstatic, wonderful, thrilling! I . . . heard myself moaning—in triumph, not in pain! There was no pain whatsoever, only a primitive and sexual elation. From my grimace, the nurse thought I was in pain and started to put the mask over my face. How annoying! In the middle of a push, I gasped, "Go away! It doesn't hurt."
>
> I felt as if I had enough strength to pull the world apart—everything was bright, illuminated. In between contractions, I shouted deliriously, "This is wonderful! My husband only wants two babies, but I want a thousand."[4]

Descent

There is still a third stage of labor, the birth of the placenta. The child is born, but the placenta, or after-birth, is yet to come. This happens within a half hour after the birth of the baby. The uterus contracts as it did pushing out the baby, and thus loosens and expels the placenta. The doctor makes sure that all the placental tissue has come out, so that the danger of the mother bleeding excessively may be avoided.

When the baby is born, it draws air into its lungs by gasping or crying. The umbilical cord is tied or clamped in two places and cut through between the clamps so that the baby is now completely on its own. The cord must be cut with sterile scissors, otherwise there is a danger of infection.

The baby can now be put to the mother's breast.

Even though there will be no milk yet, there will be some colostrum, which is good for the baby. The sucking action of the baby causes the mother's uterus to contract so that it will not bleed too much. The baby should not be given any other food, since there is enough food in its body to last until the mother's milk comes in on the second or third day.

During the next twenty-four hours, the mother needs rest and attentive care. Maria Veit, a German mother, expresses her feelings after giving birth in the following way:

> I have a child, my child—no, our child!
> And I am full of gratefulness and infinitely tired,
> This tiredness rolls over me like ocean waves,
>   as does my gratefulness and all my other thinking
>   which sinks down deep within me . . .

In Conclusion

Mrs. Ruth Heil, a registered nurse, writes: "My husband was present for the birth of our child. It was something so wonderfully beautiful, to experience those hours together, and then—the first cry! With what shall I compare such moments? It was simply the highpoint of our life together, where we sensed the power of the Creator in full depth, where we felt his almightiness, and grasped his love, and were for moments overwhelmed by his power. And to feel this together! What an impetus this is for our marriage! What we have longed for, with every heartbeat, has become reality: To understand each other completely, and to be nothing more than one body and one soul."

A conscious participation in childbirth raises the self-esteem of a woman. She doesn't need to be told who she is, doesn't need to run around searching for her true identity. She knows it.

It would have been impossible for me to write this chapter if I had not had these experiences as a mother myself. With one exception, all of our children were born in Africa. My husband was part of the "birth team," along with the wife of our missionary doctor, Alice Eastwold, to whom I am deeply indebted for passing on her own experiences in natural childbirth. Having shared the labor and birth experience will always be the highlights of our marriage for my husband and myself. Our children, also, cannot hear often enough the description of joy we experienced at their births.

VI
The Motherly Art of
Breastfeeding

Breastfeeding for the Joy of It

As I look back on my life experiences to date, those months (which combined would stretch into years) when I nursed our children were among the most satisfying and happy of my life. As Karen Pryor says: "all successful nursing mothers unite in regarding the bottle feeding mother with pity—the same pity a happily married woman feels for a frigid wife. She just doesn't know what she's missing."[1]

An Austrian mother writes: "In my opinion breastfeeding is one of the most precious gifts which God has given to a woman. For me, the nicest thing about it is to be allowed to give—the feeling of being needed. Dietrich Bonhoeffer once said: 'Nothing makes us happier than to feel that we are essentially needed by another person.' This is precisely the feeling I have when nursing one of our children. Besides that, I feel that I am giving my baby a certain security which no one else can give him. In German the word for breastfeeding is *stillen*—which means literally that the mother quiets the outward and inward needs of her child in the true sense of the word. This innermost oneness between my child and me is a unique experience."

In this chapter I would like to encourage and to comfort those mothers who feel that they are unable to breastfeed their babies. I would like to help them to have the same experience as the mother quoted above. (She, by the way, learned to breastfeed successfully only with her third child.) At the same time, I would like to challenge them to accept their motherhood to a much greater degree and to bring it to maturity—for breastfeeding is an art of the mature woman.

This is underlined also by Dr. Günter Clauser in *Die moderne Elternschule* (*A Manual for Modern Parents*):

> Breastfeeding is the continuation of the prenatal nourishment by the mother and is as much a natural process as pregnancy. . . . The inner attitude of the mother is just as important here as the milk, because it affects the basic attitude of the child with which it later faces the world. Those who have never found satisfaction at their mother's breast face this world without confidence.[2]

Nonbreastfeeding—Description of the Mother

A mother actually loses something when she does not breastfeed. What Jesus said in Luke 6:38 is certainly true here: "Give and it will be given to you; good measure, pressed down, shaken together, running over, will be put into your lap. For the measure you give will be the measure you get back."

The more she gives, the more she will receive. The more she radiates motherliness and shelteredness, the more her child will reflect gratefulness and happiness. The more she gives her child the feeling of being accepted, the more she will be able to accept herself.

If she does not breastfeed, she is losing these riches. This is true even in the physical realm. If she does not want to give milk she will not have milk. The ability to breastfeed grows with the willingness to breastfeed. The truth contained in Matthew 13:12 applies here: "For to him who has [in this connection, the willingness to breastfeed] will more be given, and he will have abundance; but from him who has not, even what he has will be taken away."

This impoverishment will affect her whole general well-being. A breastfeeding mother recovers more quickly from the strains of birth. Hormones will be set free that will make her composed and relaxed. Through the sucking at the breasts the uterus contracts and returns to its normal size. For some months no menstruation takes place. The hemoglobin count is higher. She feels completely at one with herself.

Unfortunately, not all mothers know that the more the baby sucks, the more milk will come in. This sucking should begin in the first twenty-four hours after birth. Often the baby doesn't suck enough in the first days after birth, then the mother's milk doesn't flow as freely. Temporarily her milk supply may be lessened. feed and starts to develop inferiority feelings.

In *Modern Motherhood*, Dr. Liley says: "Breastfeeding is actually such an intimate part of our human life cycle that our reaction to the question reflects our approach to life. The proportion of women who breastfeed their babies is not so much a measure of our economics or sophistication as it is of our confidence and joy in motherhood."[3]

The Drs. Newton report in the *New England Journal of Medicine*: ". . . Nursing mothers not only report sexual stimulation from suckling but also, as a group, are more interested in as rapid return to active intercourse with their husbands as possible."[4]

Sheila Kitzinger underlines this also as she writes: "Breastfeeding is a sexual activity (one reason perhaps, why some women hate it), and part of the very wide spectrum of sexuality in a woman's life, ranging all the way from her image of herself as a woman, through making love and the processes of childbearing, to the different ways in which she deals with her sons and daughters as they grow up through childhood and adolescence and her reactions to menstruation and to the menopause."[5]

Nonbreastfeeding—Deprivation of the Baby

Not only is the mother herself deprived of a rich experience, but the baby too is impoverished. As Dr. Dick Read has said: "The newborn baby has only three demands. They are warmth in the arms of its mother, food from her breast, and security in the knowledge of her presence. Breastfeeding satisfies all three."

I would like to add, nonbreastfeeding can deprive the baby of all three. First of all, this is true for the physical realm. Mother's milk is good for the baby and helps keep the baby well. The first nourishment which comes from the mother's breast is called colostrum. It is a yellowish fluid and is especially designed for the newborn. Not only is it easy for the baby to digest, but it protects it from sickness and has a laxative effect, clearing out the meconium, a dark, greenish-black, sticky substance, the first contents of the baby's bowel.

Breast milk corresponds exactly to the needs of the baby. The mother's milk is sterile and at just the right temperature for the baby. It contains certain proteins and vitamins which are necessary for the development of the child's brain and body. It is just right for the baby at every stage of its growth.

A breastfeeding mother does not have to worry about a normal baby's digestion. It takes care of itself. Children who are exclusively breastfed are never constipated, even if there is no stool for three or four days. On the other hand, soft stools are normal for breastfed babies and the mother does not have to worry about diarrhea. She can be sure that as long as she breastfeeds, all is in order.

As one doctor says, "Human milk is for the human infant. Cow's milk is for the calf." The rate of deaths among bottle-fed babies is far higher than among those who are breastfed. In the tropics a breastfed child has a chance of survival six times greater than a bottle-fed baby.

Breastfed children are healthier and have less allergies. "Dr. Robbins Kimball has observed that during the first ten years of life the breast-fed youngster is healthier and is more resistant to infections than a bottle-fed child. The bottle-fed child has '4 times the respiratory infections, 20 times the diarrhea, 22 times the miscellaneous infections, 8 times the eczema, 21 times the asthma, 27 times the hayfever, and he also had 11 times more tonsillectomies and 4 times more ear infections."[6]

A child deprived of the experience of breastfeeding is not only deprived of physical health, but also of psychological health. The baby needs the sucking satisfaction which is far greater through breastfeeding than through bottlefeeding. It is striking that in Africa where children are breastfed until they reach the age of two, there is much less neurosis in the general population.

An African psychologist, Dr. Lamba of Nigeria, says: "The newborn infant, nursed by a confident mother, experiences an unbroken state of satisfaction without effort. . . . This oral satisfaction results in re-markable self-assurance and optimism which may per-sist throughout life."

There is without any doubt a connection between nonbreastfeeding and the oral addictions of our time such as overeating, drinking, and even smoking. Chain-smoking men are certainly not masculine; neither are women who may try to imitate them. They suck like babies on their cigarettes in order to make up for that which may have been withheld from them when they were suckling infants.

The way a baby is nourished is important not only for him and his parents, but for his whole future atti-tude toward life. The German psychologist Christa Meves points out these truths: "Sucking nourishment directly from the mother's body constitutes a basic pre-supposition for the future ability to work and to love. Have we ever realized what it means for the develop-ment of the emotional life of the baby, if instead of a warm body, it receives a cold rubber nipple in its mouth?"[7]

Nonbreastfeeding—A Danger to Society

Educators have discovered that breastfed children are more adaptable and independent. In Japan, when chil-dren start school, the mother is asked if the child has been breastfed. Teachers have observed that such chil-dren are more apt to be independent and to make an easier adjustment to the new life.

That which a baby receives through its close and exclusive contact with its mother cannot be replaced later on. Therefore, children who have been separated from their mothers during the early years of their lives and who have been passed from hand to hand are apt to suffer later on from their inability to make commitments and develop qualities such as faithfulness and reliability. They will find it harder to learn from those more experienced than themselves.

Christa Meves also writes: "If a child is offered predigested food instead of motherly love and sacrifice; television instead of creative toys; being carted around in a baby-seat in the back of a car instead of tender touching, then the result will be a youth who runs wild and is hostile to the effort of creative work. This may develop into an epidemic which is menacing to the Western World."[8]

If this is true, then it is high time to ask whether the obstetric wards in our hospitals favor or hinder the spread of this epidemic. Feeding the baby according to a strict hospital schedule can often mean that the baby is so exhausted from crying that it is unable to suck when it is brought to its mother, and immediately the vicious circle starts. The mother blames herself and becomes depressed. As a result, she has no milk and in turn deprives her baby of this unique experience.

Prejudices

Inability to breastfeed is not only the result of wrong breastfeeding rules, but also of ungrounded prejudices.

It is not true:

—that the amount of milk depends upon the size of the breast;

—that breastfeeding spoils the figure (it's important to wear good brassieres and to watch your weight);

—that the inability to breastfeed is hereditary;

—that one cannot breastfeed after a Caesarean section;

—that twins cannot get enough milk if they are breastfed;

—that menstruation is a hindrance to nursing;

—that nervousness stops the production of milk (only the let-down reflex may be stopped);

—that a mother with a cold or the flu cannot breastfeed;

—that there are allergies against mother's milk (on the contrary, if the baby gets sick, it needs its mother's milk that much more, for it is the only nourishment it can accept and keep down);

—that housework is more important than the baby;

—that breastfeeding spoils the baby (on the contrary, if a baby is spared the work of sucking, then it will be spoiled).

If you baby a baby as long as it is a baby, you don't have to baby it the rest of its life.

Helps for Those Who Want to Learn to Breastfeed

Sheila Kitzinger expresses it beautifully:

> The nearest analogy to favourable conditions for the new mother to learn how to breast-feed is that provided by what are commonly considered favourable conditions for love-making: a comfortable warm bed, privacy, a relaxed atmosphere, and a sense of timeless leisure. And just as with intercourse, the first attempts may not bring the delight or satisfaction which was hoped for, so gradually the nursing couple, like the couple making love, learn to understand and respond to each other's needs; for breast-feeding, and indeed the whole of parenthood, is—like any form of loving—a process of discovery.[9]

Just as the body is prepared for pregnancy, so must the breasts be prepared for breastfeeding. It is good before birth to condition the skin of the breasts and the nipples through washing with cold water and through massage with a terry-cloth towel. It is not advisable to use soap, alcohol, or antiseptics because they may dry out the skin unnecessarily.

If a mother feels hunger or thirst, she should satisfy it. This is really the time to eat for two and to have a nourishing diet. It is also advisable to drink something before each breastfeeding.

If a mother has the feeling that her milk supply is not sufficient, she should do two things: (1) Put the baby to her breast more frequently. In the first months the baby will need to nurse from six to ten times daily. The stimulation of the breasts by frequent nursings helps to establish an adequate milk supply. On the other hand, if the baby is given a bottle, which he can drink without effort, he will suck less and less at his mother's breast and her milk supply will diminish. (2) Be alone with her baby. Sometimes a mother's milk does not flow as it should because she is not calm and relaxed. The "let-down reflex" which causes the milk to flow can be stopped if the mother is tense or distracted.

Here again is an opportunity for the father to help. If he is at home he should take care of the other children and protect her against too many well-meaning visitors so that she can be alone with her baby. If she's composed and relaxed the milk will come by itself.

Once a mother called her pediatrician because she said the child choked each time she tried to breastfeed it. Her doctor advised her to see an ear, nose, and throat specialist. The specialist said there was nothing wrong with the baby. The mother had been nursing her baby in such a way that it didn't have room to breathe through its nose! She should either sit comfortably or lie on her side with the baby lying flat beside her so that it can reach the nipple. The mother may need to make room for the baby to breathe by pressing her breast gently away at this point.

One should never pull the nipple from the baby's mouth, for this will cause tissue damage and even pain for the mother. By inserting the little finger into the baby's mouth beside the nipple, the suction is broken and the baby lets go readily.

In case there is nipple soreness, one should not limit the sucking time. Pain is greatest during the first few pulls on the nipple and seldom lasts more than a few seconds. It usually clears up by itself in two or three days. The mother must always wash her hands with soap and water before touching her breasts. Especially in the early weeks after childbirth, the nipples must be kept just as clean and dry as possible; otherwise a breast infection can develop. If this should happen, the mother should be careful to let the baby nurse first at the sore breast to be sure it will not become too full. A good ointment and letting the nipple air after the baby has nursed may also help.

I know from my own experience that the best help for successful breastfeeding is the assistance and encouragement of another woman, possibly of the same age group, who has breastfed successfully. Equally important is the readiness to learn. There are women who learn the art of breastfeeding gradually from baby to baby. One German mother, who just wrote to me, said, "It was only when my fifth baby was five weeks old that I succeeded in breastfeeding completely and now we are a happy 'nursing couple'."

In Dr. Dana Raphael's book *The Tender Gift: Breastfeeding*, I found her use of the word "doula" (it comes from the Greek, and in Aristotle's time meant "slave") to be most helpful. The "doula" is the one who mothers the mother. "Her very presence gives the mother a better chance of remaining calm and nursing her baby. . . .

Whatever she does is less important than the fact that she *is there*. The doula can also be a man—one who though inexperienced shows a willingness and ability to be supportive."[10]

Breastfeeding is such a joyful experience that it can actually serve as an incentive to have more children. In fact, that is the only "hazard" of which I can think. Today one can meet parents who have actually developed an inferiority complex because they have not complied with the accepted two-child standard of our society. It would be better that some couples have no children if they have them grudgingly. Others, gifted for parenthood, should have half a dozen.

A child who is not breastfed is, of course, not condemned to failure. It may only have a more difficult time adjusting to certain situations in life. Children who cannot be breastfed need the uninterrupted closeness of the mother and frequent skin contact that much more. They should be held close to the breast even when they drink from the bottle.

Weaning, Also an Art

The time of weaning is decided by the baby and not by the relatives. This can be around nine months or even later, as many modern mothers are discovering.

Dr. Ashley Montagu is of the opinion that the human baby is actually born nine months too soon, but his brain is growing so quickly that at a later date, his head could not pass through the birth canal. Not before nine months after birth, that is about eighteen months after conception, is a baby fully mature. This period of time corresponds to the time of breastfeeding. After nine months of age babies become more independent, learn to drink from a cup, and lose interest in the breast.

At this age, breastfeeding is, above all, of psychological importance. Even longer than it needs nourishment from the mother, the baby needs the feeling of being close and sheltered.

It is important to wean a baby gradually in order not to disturb the child emotionally. A wise mother begins to offer her baby a few spoonsful of cereal around six months or even earlier. She can give her baby fruit juice and a mashed ripe banana when it is a few months old. By the time a baby is a year old it can eat many of the adult foods as well as drink from a cup. As soon as the baby is eating enough other foods, the mother should breastfeed it only if it expressly wants to. This will usually be the case just before the baby goes to bed, when it is sick, or when it needs comfort for another reason.

If a mother feels she should initiate weaning it should never be done abruptly. The weaning from the breast is a kind of second birth in the sense that it means a second separation from the mother. This second separation for the baby (and for the mother too) may be even harder than the first one at the time of birth. It is well to remember that it is one of the most difficult times in a baby's life, when it needs special love and understanding from both father and mother. Initially a baby stops nursing when he or she is ready.

The "Nursing" Father

Here I would like to say a word about the father during the time of breastfeeding. Certainly it is not easy for him during this time to fulfill the double role of being husband of his wife and father of his child. He may often feel like an outsider, and yet mother and baby need him very much. He too can nurse! Not physically, of course, but psychologically. It is important for the small baby that the father be present—that the baby see him, hear him, feel him. "If a man knows how to handle a woman tenderly, he should be able to handle a baby. A woman has only to think of the pleasure her husband can give her to realize he has his own kind of sensitivity and gentleness," says Sheila Kitzinger.[11]

Dr. Bradley says that he has rarely seen a successful breastfeeding mother, unless she was supported by her husband.

However, if he is jealous, supporting the popular opinion that breasts are for the father and not for the baby, or if he has joined the choir of those who try to persuade the mother that she does not have enough milk and "just can't do it," then the milk will stop and she will indeed become unable to nurse.

On the other hand, if he really believes in his wife and encourages her to master the art of breastfeeding; protects her from disturbances, excitement, and visitors; cares for the children and teaches them to take over some of the mother's work; tells his wife that she is beautiful when she breastfeeds; then the milk will come and, in effect, the father nurses his child by nursing the mother.

Unfortunately, some young and inexperienced mothers often make the mistake of discouraging fathers who are willing to "nurse." If the baby becomes the center of their lives and actually more important to them than their husbands, then they should not be surprised if their husbands feel neglected, become jealous and even try to find comfort and understanding in the arms of another woman. It is like a German father who complained, "As far as my wife is concerned, the baby gets better treatment than the husband."

In spite of all the love for the child, it should not take over the first place in the family. If I tell African mothers not to forget that their husbands are still Number One, they click their tongues in disapproval. In spite of their disapproval, Madame Ernestine Banyolak from Cameroun has the courage to say to her African sisters,

"Children are guests in the family. They come, stay for awhile and then leave again. Husband and wife, however, remain together." This experience that father and mother belong together is of great importance for the small child. Education for marriage begins in the second month of a baby's life. Therefore, the father should be in the picture from the very beginning. This truth seems to be forgotten today by those who claim that also the unmarried woman has a right to have a baby. The baby has a greater right to have a father.

In summary, if a wife wants her husband to treat her like a queen and to "nurse" her, then she must treat the father like a king and "nurse" him.

This brings up the question of sexual relations during the time of nursing. After childbirth most doctors advise a couple to wait from three to six weeks before having intercourse. It takes this long for a mother's uterus to return to its normal state and for an episiotomy to heal completely if she has had one. Also, there is a red discharge from the uterus after the baby is born, which is called the lochia. It lasts about two weeks and tends to flow most when the mother is nursing her baby. This is a good thing because it means the uterus is contracting and returning to its normal state. Later the lochia becomes a lighter color and then it finally stops. If the mother notices that the red flow returns once it has lightened, it usually means that she is overworking. When this happens, she needs to rest and nurse her baby often, which causes the uterus to contract and the flow to cease.

Three weeks after a normal delivery, a breastfeeding mother can have intercourse until there are signs of mucus. The quantity and the quality of the milk will not be affected. The father's sperm cannot enter into the milk and cause the baby to get sick—an opinion which is still widespread in many parts of the world.

On the contrary, as I have emphasized before, the

best way for a father to show his love to his child is to love the baby's mother. It is even true that mothers who breastfeed their babies are more interested than non-breastfeeding mothers in returning to active intercourse. It may be for many a way to show the father of their child their gratefulness and love. At the same time, they share with their child the experience of fatherly protection. The husband, however, experiences when "nursing" his wife that he is nursed and appeased himself and that he need not be jealous of his baby. This sharing and mutuality of nursing is perhaps the deepest dimension of oneness between husband and wife during this period.

Breastfeeding and Child-Spacing

This is one of the most difficult questions and all the answers have not yet been found. Medical research needs here the help of breastfeeding mothers.

It is ordinarily the case that the sucking action of the baby at the mother's breast prevents ovulation. As long as no ovulation takes place, no new conception is possible. This is usually true only as long as the mother is completely breastfeeding her baby. Total breastfeeding means that she nurses him six to eight times a day, according to the needs of the baby, and does not give him any solids. Besides this, no pacifier should be offered to the baby because he will suck that much less at the mother's breast. Under these conditions 86% of women do not ovulate during the first three months after birth.

Normally the first menstruation of breastfeeding mothers is a so-called withdrawal bleeding, which means that it was not preceded by an ovulation. This will be the case for 95 percent of mothers who are totally breastfeeding. Their first menstruation will not be preceded by an ovulation.

African women, who according to their traditional custom resume intercourse with their husbands after the first menstruation, have often told me, "I had my period only once after our baby began to walk and then I was pregnant again." What had happened? Just during the months when these women were infertile, because they were breastfeeding completely and neither menstruation nor ovulation took place, they abstained from intercourse. In other words, they had abstained during the whole time when they could not conceive, and just at the moment when they had their first ovulation, they had intercourse and became pregnant again. In the Yoruba tribe in Nigeria a study has shown that the average length of time before women who were completely breastfeeding had their menstrual period after childbirth was sixteen months.

In addition to what I mentioned in the second chapter, I would like to share the following directives:

The mother who does not breastfeed completely has to reckon with the possibility of a conception beginning with the fourth week after childbirth. Three weeks after the delivery, she should start to take her waking temperature again and not wait for the first menstruation.

A mother who breastfeeds completely should start to take her temperature eight weeks after the delivery and to watch for the symptoms of ovulation—cervical mucus and midpain. Since the cycle may be irregular in the beginning, and often without ovulation, observing these symptoms is especially important. Only after the symptoms have disappeared (cessation of the cervical fertile mucus) and the temperature has been at a higher level for at least three days and remains at a high level can she be certain that the infertile days have started.

Little is known about the time before ovulation after the first menstruation while the mother is breastfeeding—therefore abstention during this part of the cycle is advisable. The Drs. Billings from Australia have found that the so-called dry days before ovulation, when no cervical mucus can be observed, are infertile. A helpful book giving more information about this is Sheila Kippley's *Breastfeeding and Natural Child Spacing: The Ecology of Natural Mothering*, Harper & Row.

Breastfeeding and Working

From all I have said so far, it is evident that breastfeeding and fulltime work outside the home are not easy to manage. Many women seem to have the idea that the time spent taking care of a baby is actually lost time and they can barely wait until they get this "messy" period out of the way as soon as possible in order to be free for something more important. A baby feels this. It needs the undivided attention and uninterrupted presence of its mother, who cannot be replaced by anyone else—not even by the dearest aunt or grandmother.

No woman should be ashamed of being "only" a housewife or mother. On the contrary, she should be proud and should know that by renouncing an outside job when her children are young she renders an invaluable service to her baby and to society as a whole. She also should remember that this period where she gives herself entirely to her baby is relatively short and she should consider its importance for the future life of her child. When she looks back she is apt to see this time of the "nursing couple" as being among the richest moments of her life when she was most fulfilled and happiest.

If other people try to tell her that other things are more important, she should listen to her motherly instinct which gives her the feeling for what is right. It is not right to entrust her helpless child to any other person. Otherwise, the child may never develop values such as love, gratefulness, reliability, and responsibility, as the biographies of juvenile delinquents prove in abundance. In contrast, when one looks into the early life of a person who has made a real contribution to mankind, one will mostly find a good and positive mother-child relationship at the beginning.

For many mothers in America, this "feeling for what is right" is being pushed more and more into the foreground. One example is the movement of La Leche League. Since its beginning in the United States with two mothers in 1956, 1,919 La Leche groups with 5,997 leaders in thirty-two countries have been organized. Their motto is "Good mothering through breastfeeding the world over." Their members have rediscovered what African mothers knew all along: the nonbreastfeeding mother deprives herself of a possibility of loving herself as a woman.

Of course, here again it is true that even the most intelligent and convincing arguments of a psychological or a biological nature are of no avail unless they get across to the woman that instinctive feeling for what is right, and open to her this dimension of being a woman. In the final analysis, the art of breastfeeding has its roots in the peace a mother finds with God.

It is significant that in the Psalms peace with God is illustrated by a child quieted at its mother's breast:

But I have calmed and quieted my soul,
 like a child quieted at its mother's breast;
 like a child that is quieted is my soul.
Psalm 131:1-2

VII
Menopause—Chance for
a New Beginning

The menopause—the so-called change of life—does not mean that femininity is lost, but exactly the contrary; that femininity is regained and rediscovered. Once again, a new and unexpected dimension is added to the joy of being a woman. The change of life is not the end of life.

Many women are tempted to think this. With fear they keep their eyes fixed on the time when they will see the first symptoms and then they give up all hope. They let themselves go—also in their outward appearance. To put it bluntly, they become old instead of mature. There are only these two possibilities.

But in order to become mature we must face again the task of self-acceptance and self-affirmation. In the ripeness of life, it is more important than ever consciously to love oneself as a woman. As Dr. Marion Hilliard has put it: "The change can begin at 45, but life begins at 50."

Dr. Bovet in *A Handbook to Marriage* relate
touching story about his wife after many years of marriage. Once while gazing upon his sleeping wife, he took
notice of the different character lines in her counte-
nance. She was not old, but she had some wrinkles in
her face. The little wrinkles above her eyebrows appeared whenever she asked a witty question. When
thinking deeply, she wrinkled the middle of her brow
causing vertical lines in her forehead. The deeper hori-
zontal wrinkles were etched in her forehead when he
was sick and she was worried about their future. He
noticed the wrinkles at the corners of her eyes which
radiated love when looking at their child. At the corner
of her mouth were little wrinkles which appeared whenever she noticed a funny animal. She would laughingly
say, "Our Lord God certainly had a sense of humor that
he would create such a comical animal." The more in-
tently he gazed upon her face, the memories of their
years together swept over him and he saw into her very
being. Indeed, her precious face contained in shorthand
her whole biography.

Just as with every stage of life, the time after menopause also has its special beauty. "My, you are beautiful!" said a young man to a white-haired lady. "Why
shouldn't I be?" came the answer, "After all, I'm sev-
enty-three!"

First of all, we must understand what happens biologically to a woman. The production of the female
hormone estrogen recedes and the hormone of motherhood, progesterone, stops almost completely. On the
other hand, there is a greater production of other sex
hormones which lead to an augmented ability of sexual
response.

This process happens mostly during the years between forty-five and fifty. Some women—probably two-
thirds—don't notice anything at all, others suffer more

...sion, insomnia, headaches, and skin
...gaps can occur and emotional reac-
...e stronger.

...n are overcome by an extreme tiredness.
...ree periods of life when a woman is espe-
c... ...: during puberty, during the first three
month... pregnancy, and during menopause.

Menopause is not a loss and therefore no reason to be depressed, since the feeling of depression often accompanies a feeling of loss. "Everything is just as it was before," said a woman dentist to me, "only nicer because after menopause there are no more menstrual periods."

Among the things that can become more beautiful are the marital relations. The cessation of the production of certain hormones has nothing to do with sexual desire, which can become, as mentioned above, even stronger. There are women who reach climax only in the time after menopause.

Of course, this joy, not only in sexual union but in life as a whole, depends a lot upon the attitude a woman has toward herself during and after menopause. Most women need to work on this. The last thing a woman needs now is pity—let alone self-pity. What she needs is a lot of humor, playful serenity, and the ability to laugh, even about herself. She needs to know that she is able to reach a plateau of constancy and stability as never before, which allows her to rely upon her body, her will power, and her emotions.

This work on herself means that she does not "let herself go"—this expression hits the nail on the head—but that she "comes to herself," clings to herself and puts her arms around herself. This means that she dresses tastefully and preserves a healthy "self-esteem." Anne Morrow Lindbergh says in *Gift from the Sea*: "Perhaps one can at last in middle age, if not earlier, be completely oneself. And what a liberation that would be!"[1]

She should watch her weight especially now. This depends upon three factors: her constitution, her diet, and her physical exercise. The temptation to do less and eat more is especially great. A daily swim and walk are better for her than swallowing hormone pills.

She should give in to the tiredness, however, and allow herself more sleep and rest, even if she is still working. She has to realize that she is now going through a sort of puberty in reverse, in which only two-thirds of her usual energy are available to her. In the struggle between a willing spirit with high goals and an exhausted body, the body always wins—unless its demand for rest is satisfied.

This demand cannot be satisfied only by sleep, but also by a day off now and then for complete relaxation —maybe in another place—a Finnish sauna, a new hairdo, a leisurely cup of coffee in a nice café or restaurant, an evening with good friends or a concert. One should not underestimate the importance of these little things. For the working woman, careful planning of her weekend needs special attention.

The greatest help, however, is a task which challenges her, to which she can give herself completely and which gives her the feeling of growing and of being needed. Such a task could be, for example, to become a *doula*, which Dr. Raphael has defined in her book *The Tender Gift* as mothering a younger mother.

In the same vein, the apostle Paul writes to Titus: "Bid the older women likewise to be reverent in behavior, not to be slanderers or slaves to drink; *they are to teach what is good and so train the young women to love their husbands and children.*" Her heart and her eyes should be open to her surroundings and she should know that the older she becomes, the more important are the people around her. They are her greatest support in her battle against self-pity.

If she accepts the challenge of a task, then the word "menopause" loses its menacing connotation. It becomes a possibility for a new beginning and a heightened feeling for life which she is now able to see more soberly, more realistically, not overestimating it nor demanding too much of herself.

In an article called "Change of Life," Dr. Agathe Burki of Switzerland says: "Crisis is transition, change, birth of something new. The future which God opens up has to be realized step by step. Something new is offered, but it costs a price: One has to let go of the old. Life is lived no longer in its breadth, but in its depth. Another dimension has to take the upper hand."

To help realize these goals, Dr. Burki makes the following practical suggestions:

—Change your habits of life. It's time to renew your furniture, or at least to move it around. Being prepared for something new does not only mean accepting it, but also getting up and going toward it.

—Sort out your possessions. Get rid of old books, souvenirs, letters which have lost their meaning. The dead weight or junk which is disposed of allows room for new things. Only those things should remain which have stood the test of time and space.

—If there's an unfulfilled desire, now is the time to make it a reality. If circumstances allow it, take that trip you've dreamed about all your life. Perhaps there's still an old desire from childhood which should be fulfilled in order to outgrow it and to be able to put it aside. Maybe you will discover that such old desires don't taste so good after all. There are dreams which make us happy and cheerful, but there are others which become a constant source of dissatisfaction—and they should be gradually eliminated.

—Renew old friendships, cultivate them, and take up new ones. Often during one's prime working years friendships are neglected. However, one needs friends in order to give and to receive. The church congregation to which you belong and where each one learns and practices giving and receiving will become more meaningful.

—Practice being alone. Only the one who is able to be alone is able to be a good friend to others and to make a contribution when in fellowship with others. It's not always easy to be alone. Try reading, taking up a hobby or handcraft, listening to music, embroidering, knitting, or painting. This time could also be used to read the Bible, study it, and converse in solitude with God.

—Finally, there is the possibility that, after years of suffering and struggling, certain problems remain unsolved. During the change of life, the moment has come to seek out another person to whom you can open up all that is hidden who can help you to find freedom and order.

In closing this book, I would like to endorse this last suggestion with a personal testimony. What has helped me most during crisis periods in my life has been the confession of sins and the acceptance of personally proclaimed forgiveness. By accepting God's offer in Christ, "Come unto me all you that labor and are heavy-laden, and I will give you rest," I have received each time renewed ability to accept and to love myself as a woman.

A Final Word

After having read this book, some may feel as though they have been cast on shore after a shipwreck. To those who feel this way, I would like to say two things:

First, I could write this book only because I have been shipwrecked many times myself.

Second, the message is that Christ *has* redeemed us. This message is especially for those who feel as if they have failed and are shipwrecked. We cannot redeem ourselves through our own endeavors and by "trying harder." But we can open up our empty hands and stretch them out.

Empty hands are the only ones which God can fill. Hilde Domin has delicately expressed it, saying: "Reach out your hand as you would to a bird—gently, imperceptibly—to receive the wonder—the miracle."

Appendix A

International Federation for Promotion of Family Life

Basic Principles*

Man in the modern world has many individual and social responsibilities. To help him to face these responsibilities maturely and freely he needs information and education.

The present rate of growth of world population underlines man's responsibilities in the area of sexuality. Fertility control is not the sole solution to this problem. Social reforms, economic development and the raising of the living standards also play an important if not a primary role.

Our organization is based on a belief in man's need of education in order to grow in freedom, self–knowledge and responsibility to his full potential as a human person.

The following principles and attitudes express further this belief:

* For further information, write: Human Life Foundation, 1776 K Street, N.W., Washington, D.C. 20006.

1. The family unit, which is vital for the development of society, has three essential elements: *man* as a person, husband, father; *woman* as a person, wife, mother; *child* present actually or potentially, to be respected as a person from conception.

2. Growth as a person is a gradual and continuing process. The surmounting of difficulties seems to be a necessary part of this process. This applies to all aspects of the person including sexuality.

3. The components of human sexuality, whether physical, spiritual, psychological or procreational need to be understood and integrated by man in every stage of life. In this context human sexuality is best expressed in loving interpersonal relationships.

4. For a married couple a loving, generous, faithful and stable relationship promotes their security as persons and that of their children. Knowledge of themselves and each other promotes this relationship. The responsibility of conception regulation is inherent in this relationship.

5. The process of education should be understood as a sharing of information in the framework of a dialogue which is simultaneously a listening to and acceptance of each other on an equal basis (person to person, or couple to couple). Thus the couple becomes responsible not only for the application of a technique of conception regulation but for a way of life freely chosen.

6. In this context, natural family planning is defined as a dialogue leading to responsible parenthood based on an educated awareness and acceptance of the cyclic phases of fertility and infertility, and loving abstinence in married life becomes basic to this dialogue.

7. Our organization respects and accepts spiritual values, from whatever source, which may deepen the understanding and sustain the purpose of a person or a couple.

Bibliography

"Amour et Famille." Fiches Documentaires du Centre de Liason des Equipes de Recherche, No. 71. Paris, 1972.

Ancelle. *Mystère du Couple.* Paris: Les Editions Ouvrières, 1964.

Berne, Eric. *Sex in Human Loving.* New York: Simon & Schuster, 1970.

Bird, Joseph and Lois. *Love is All.* Garden City, N.Y.: Doubleday, 1968.

————. *The Freedom of Sexual Love.* New York: Doubleday, 1967.

Boston Women's Health Book Collective. *Our Bodies, Ourselves—A Book for and about Women.* New York: Simon and Schuster, 1974.

Bovet, Theodor. *A Handbook to Marriage.* New York: Doubleday, 1958.

Bradley, Robert, M.D. *Husband–Coached Childbirth.* New York: Harper & Row, 1965.

Clausser, Günter, M.D. *Die Moderne Elternschule.* Freiburg: Herder Verlag, 1969.

Défossez, Marie Paule. *Vivre au feminin.* Paris: Editions du Centurion, 1971.

Deutsch, Ronald M. *The Key to Feminine Response in Marriage*. New York: Ballantine Books, Inc., 1968.

Fisher, Seymour. *The Female Orgasm*. New York: Basic Books, Inc., 1973.

Guardini, Romano. *Die Annahme seiner Selbst*. Wurzburg: Werkbuch 5. Auflage, 1969.

Hammarskjold, Dag. *Markings*. London: Faber and Faber, 1964.

Hulme, William E. *Building a Christian Marriage*. Minneapolis, Minn.: Augsburg, 1965.

Kegel, A. H. "Stress Incontinence and Genital Relaxation." Ciba Symposium, February-March, 1952.

————. "Sexual Functions of the Pubococcygeus Muscle." Western Journal of Surgery, Obstetrics and Gynecology, 1952.

————. "Stress Incontinence of Urine in Women; Physiologic Treatment." Journal of the International College of Surgeons, April, 1965.

Kippley, John and Sheila, *The Art of Natural Family Planning*, Couple to Couple League International Inc. P. O. Box 11084, Cincinnati, Ohio 45211, 1975.

Kippley, Sheila. *Breast-feeding and Natural Child Spacing*. New York: Harper & Row, 1974.

Kitzinger, Sheila. *Giving Birth*. New York: Taplinger Publishing Co., 1971.

La Leche League, International 1963 "The Womanly Art of Breast Feeding." 9619 Minneapolis Ave., Franklin Park, Illinois, 60131.

Liley, Margaret, M.D. with Beth Day. *Modern Motherhood*. New York: Random House, Inc, 1967.

Meves, Christa. *Manipulierte Masslosigkeit*. Freiburg: Herderbücherei 401, 1971.

Meves, Christa and Joachim Illies. *Lieben, Was ist Das?* Freiburg: Herderbücherei 362, 1972.

Millman & Goldman. *Modern Women, Her Psychology and Sexuality*. Springfield, Illinois: Thomas Publishers, 1969.

Morgan, Marabel. *The Total Woman*. Old Tappen, N.J.: Fleming H. Revell, 1973.

Mount, Eric Jr. *The Feminine Factor*. Richmond, Virginia: John Knox Press, 1973.

Newton, Prof. Niles. "The Point of View of the Consumer." The National Childbirth Trust, Newsletter 23, 1973.

Pryor, Karen. *Nursing Your Baby*. New York: Harper & Row, 1963.

Raphael, Dana. *The Tender Gift: Breastfeeding*. Englewood Cliffs, N.J.: Prentice-Hall, Inc., 1973.

Roetzer, Joseph. *Kinderzahl und Liebesehe*. 7th edition. Vienna: Herder Verlag, 1972.

Scanzoni, Letha and Nancy Hardesty. *All We're Meant To Be*. Waco, Texas: Word Books, 1974.

Serena. "Love and Life—Fertility and Conception Prevention." Ottawa, Canada: Serena, 1974. This very helpful booklet can be obtained directly from Serena, 55 Parkdale Ave., Ottawa, Ontario K1Y 1E5.

Trobisch, Walter. *I Married You*. New York: Harper & Row, 1971.

Wessel, Helen. *Natural Childbirth and the Family*. New York: Harper & Row, 1973.

Notes

Chapter I

1. Romano Guardini, "Die Annahme seiner Selbst" (Werkbuch, Wuerzburg, 1969), p. 14.
2. Boston Women's Health Book Collective, *Our Bodies, Ourselves—A Book For and About Women* (New York: Simon and Schuster, 1973), p. 3.

Chapter II

1. Ancelle, Mystère du Couple (Paris: Les Editions Ouvrières, 1967), p. 15.
2. *Modern Woman, Her Psychology and Sexuality* (Springfield, Ill.: Schaefer, Thomas Publishers, 1969), p. 170–171.
3. Joseph W. Bird and Lois F. Bird, *The Freedom of Sexual Love* (New York: Doubleday & Company, 1967), pp. 137–138.
4. Ronald M. Deutsch, *The Key to Feminine Response*

in Marriage (New York: Ballantine Books, 1968), p. 14.

5. Paul Popenoe, *Marital Counselling with Special Reference to Frigidity* (American Institute of Family Relations Publication No. 502, Los Angeles, California).

6. Deutsch, *op. cit.*, p. 15.

7. *Ibid.*, pp. 15–16.

8. *Ibid.*, p. 176.

9. Eric Berne, *Sex in Human Loving* (New York: Simon and Shuster, 1970), p. 43–44.

10. Dag Hammarskjöld, *Markings*, trans. Sjöberg and Auden (London: Faber and Faber, 1964), p. 54.

11. Seymour Fisher, *The Female Orgasm* (New York: Basic Books, 1973), p. 331.

12. Theodor Bovet, *A Handbook to Marriage* (Garden City, N.Y.: Doubleday & Company, Dolphin Book, 1958), p. 64.

13. William E. Hulme, *Building a Christian Marriage* (Minneapolis, Minnesota: Augsburg, 1965), pp. 92–93.

14. Joseph and Lois Bird, *Love Is All* (Garden City, N.Y.: Doubleday & Company, 1968), pp. 70–74.

CHAPTER III

1. Seymour Fisher, *The Female Orgasm* (New York: Basic Books, 1973), p. 129.

2. Sheila Kippley, *Breast-feeding and Natural Child Spacing* (New York: Harper & Row, 1974), p. 76.

3. Josef Roetzer, M.D., *Kinderzahl and Liebesehe* (Vienna: Herder & Co., 1972), pp. 26–27.

4. *Ibid.*, pp. 24–25.

5. *Ibid.*, pp. 31–32.

6. *Amour et Famille*, Fiches Documentaires du Centre de Liaison des Équipes de Récherche, No. 71 (Paris, 1972).

CHAPTER IV

1. Joseph and Lois Bird, *Love Is All* (Garden City, N.Y.: Doubleday & Company, 1968), p. 85.
2. Margaret Liley, M.D., and Beth Day, *Modern Motherhood* (New York: Random House, 1967), p. 4.

CHAPTER V

1. Niles Newton, "The Point of View of the Consumer," The National Childbirth Trust, 9 Queensborough Terrace, Bays Water, London W23TB, Newsletter 23 (Spring 1973), p. 3.
2. Sheila Kitzinger, *Giving Birth* (New York: Taplinger Publishing Co., 1971), pp. 26–27.
3. *Ibid.*
4. Helen Wessel, *Natural Childbirth and the Family* (New York: Harper & Row, 1973), p. 273.

CHAPTER VI

1. Karen Pryor, *Nursing Your Baby* (New York: Harper & Row, 1963), p. 4.
2. Günter Clauser, M.D. *Die moderne Elternschule* (Freiberg: Herder, 1969), p. 120.
3. Margaret Liley, M.D., and Beth Day, *op. cit.*, p. 19.
4. Michael and Niles Newton, M.D., Ph.D., "New England Journal of Medicine," November 30, 1967.
5. Sheila Kitzinger, *Giving Birth* (New York: Taplinger Publishing Co., 1971), p. 187.
6. Sheila Kippley, *Breast-feeding and Natural Child Spacing* (New York: Harper & Row, 1974), p. 106.
7. Christa Meves and Joachim Illies, *Lieben, Was ist Das?* (Freiburg: Herder Bücherei, Vol. 362, 1972), p. 26.
8. Christa Meves, *Manipulierte Masslosigkeit* (Freiburg: Herder Bücherei, Vol. 401, 1971), p. 27.

9. Kitzinger, *op. cit.*, p. 187.
10. Kitzinger, *op. cit.*, p. 180.

CHAPTER VII

1. Anne Morrow Lindbergh, *Gift from the Sea* (New York: Signet Books, 1955), p. 82.

Appendix B

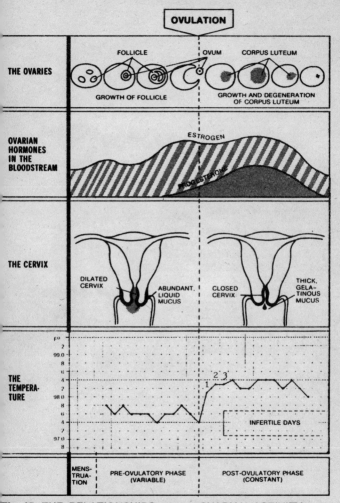

Fig. 15 THE RELATIONSHIPS among OVARIAN ACTIVITY, OVARIAN HORMONES, the CERVIX, and the TEMPERATURE during the menstrual cycle.